GoodFood
More veggie dish

D0657489

10 9 8 7 6 5 4 3 2 1

Published in 2012 by BBC Books, an imprint of Ebury Publishing.
A Random House Group Company

The Random House Group Limited
Reg. No. 954009

Addresses for companies within the Random House Group can be found at
www.randomhouse.co.uk

A CIP catalogue record for this book is available from the British Library.

The Random House Group Limited supports The Forest Stewardship Council (FSC®), the leading international forest certification organisation. Our books carrying the FSC label are printed on FSC® certified paper. FSC is the only forest certification scheme endorsed by the leading environmental organisations, including Greenpeace. Our paper procurement policy can be found at www.randomhouse.co.uk/environment

To buy books by your favourite authors and register for offers visit www.randomhouse.co.uk

Printed and bound by Firmengruppe APPL, aprinta druck, Wemding, Germany
Colour reproduction by Dot Gradations Ltd, UK

Commissioning editor: Muna Reyal
Project editor: Sarah Watling
Designer: Kathryn Gammon
Production: Rebecca Jones
Picture researcher: Gabby Harrington

ISBN: 9781849905329

MIX
Paper from
responsible sources
FSC™ C004592

Picture credits

BBC *Good Food* magazine would like to thank the following people for providing photos. While every effort has been made to trace and acknowledge all photographers we should like to apologise should there be any errors or omissions.

Peter Cassidy p33, p51, p91, p101, p107, p155, p161, p181, p183; Will Heap p13, p25, p35, p45, p47, p49, p55, p57, p61, p63, p87, p113, p115, p119, p143, p191, p201, p211, p209; Amanda Heywood p43, p121; William Lingwood p79; Gareth Morgans p21, p73, p89, p145, p168, 171, p175, p195; David Munns p15, p19, p27, p53, p71, p83, p85, p95, p131, p135, p139, p157, p163, p165, p173, p177, p187, p193, p207; Myles New p17, p93, p111, p125, p133, p141, p147, p149, p153, p179; Stuart Ovenden p23, p31, p37, p159, p205; Lis Parsons p67, p69, p75, p77, p99, p127, p167, p185, p189, p199; Charlie Richards p29, p39, p59, p105, p203; Roger Stowell p41, p65; Yuki Sugiura p117, p123, p129, p151; Dawie Verwey p81; Philip Webb p11, p97, p103, p109, p137, p197

All the recipes in this book were created by the editorial team at *Good Food* and by regular contributors to BBC magazines.

everyday

GoodFood
More veggie dishes

Editor **Sharon Brown**

BOOKS

Contents

Introduction

Vegetarian food has never been more delicious! Gone are the days when all a veggie could expect was a mushroom omelette. Supermarkets and markets are now full of an ever-increasing range of both home-grown and exotic fruit and veg and all sorts of other exciting ingredients with which to make enticing suppers and main meals.

Although the recipes in this book have been specially devised for vegetarians, they are also ideal for the increasing numbers of people who aren't strict vegetarians but simply choose to eat less meat in their diets.

Food manufacturers are aware of the elements that make up a vegetarian diet and so they try to label their products in detail to make shopping easier for veggies, but it's always worth checking labels. Many cheeses are now suitable for vegetarians as they do not use animal rennet in the production. Parmesan, however, is always made with calf rennet, but you can buy similar-style hard cheeses that are ok for vegetarians, so look out for them when shopping.

This book is packed with all the favourite veggie dishes from *Good Food* magazine. Here you'll find supper solutions made in just 30 minutes, such as *Spring vegetable tagliatelle with lemon sauce* and *Tomato & goat's cheese couscous*; there are also family favourites including *Veggie shepherd's pie with sweet potato mash* and *Butternut macaroni cheese*; new salad ideas, and special meals to impress family and friends – just try the wonderful *Pumpkin, cranberry & red onion tagine*. All the recipes have been triple-tested in the *Good Food* test kitchen so success – and fabulous flavours – are guaranteed every time!

Sharon

Sharon Brown

Notes and conversion tables

NOTES ON THE RECIPES
- Eggs are large in the UK and Australia and extra large in America unless stated otherwise.
- Wash fresh produce before preparation.
- Recipes contain nutritional analyses for 'sugar', which means the total sugar content including all natural sugars in the ingredients, unless otherwise stated.

OVEN TEMPERATURES

Gas	°C	°C Fan	°F	Oven temp.
¼	110	90	225	Very cool
½	120	100	250	Very cool
1	140	120	275	Cool or slow
2	150	130	300	Cool or slow
3	160	140	325	Warm
4	180	160	350	Moderate
5	190	170	375	Moderately hot
6	200	180	400	Fairly hot
7	220	200	425	Hot
8	230	210	450	Very hot
9	240	220	475	Very hot

APPROXIMATE WEIGHT CONVERSIONS
- All the recipes in this book list both imperial and metric measurements. Conversions are approximate and have been rounded up or down. Follow one set of measurements only; do not mix the two.
- Cup measurements, which are used by cooks in Australia and America, have not been listed here as they vary from ingredient to ingredient. Kitchen scales should be used to measure dry/solid ingredients.

Good Food are concerned about sustainable sourcing and animal welfare. Where possible humanely reared meats, sustainably caught fish (see fishonline. org for further information from the Marine Conservation Society) and free-range chickens and eggs are used when recipes are originally tested.

SPOON MEASURES

Spoon measurements are level unless otherwise specified.

- 1 teaspoon (tsp) = 5ml
- 1 tablespoon (tbsp) = 15ml
- 1 Australian tablespoon = 20ml (cooks in Australia should measure 3 teaspoons where 1 tablespoon is specified in a recipe)

APPROXIMATE LIQUID CONVERSIONS

metric	imperial	AUS	US
50ml	2fl oz	¼ cup	¼ cup
125ml	4fl oz	½ cup	½ cup
175ml	6fl oz	¾ cup	¾ cup
225ml	8fl oz	1 cup	1 cup
300ml	10fl oz/½ pint	½ pint	1¼ cups
450ml	16fl oz	2 cups	2 cups/1 pint
600ml	20fl oz/1 pint	1 pint	2½ cups
1 litre	35fl oz/1¾ pints	1¾ pints	1 quart

Moroccan spiced cauliflower & almond soup

When cauliflowers are cheap and plentiful in the shops and markets, make a batch of this soup and freeze it. It's deliciously creamy with a spicy kick.

TAKES 30 MINUTES ● SERVES 4

1 large cauliflower
2 tbsp olive oil
½ tsp each ground cinnamon, cumin and coriander
2 tbsp harissa paste, plus extra to garnish
1 litre/1¾ pints hot vegetable stock
50g/2oz toasted flaked almonds, plus extra to garnish

1 Cut the cauliflower into small florets.
2 Heat the oil in a large pan, add the spices and harissa paste, and fry for 2 minutes. Add the cauliflower florets, hot vegetable stock and almonds. Cover and cook for 20 minutes until the cauliflower is tender.
3 Blend the soup until smooth, then serve in warmed bowls with an extra drizzle of harissa and a sprinkle of toasted almonds on top.

PER SERVING 200 kcals, protein 8g, carbs 8g, fat 16g, sat fat 2g, fibre 3g, sugar 3g, salt 2.7g

Italian vegetable soup

*This hearty soup, packed with vegetables and Italian flavours, is a meal in itself.
You can freeze it for up to 3 months before adding the cheese and pasta.*

TAKES 45 MINUTES • SERVES 8

2 onions, chopped
2 carrots, chopped
4 celery sticks, chopped
1 tbsp olive oil
2 tbsp sugar
4 garlic cloves, crushed
2 tbsp tomato purée
2 bay leaves
few thyme sprigs
3 courgettes, chopped
400g can butter beans, rinsed and
    drained
400g can chopped tomatoes
1.2 litres/2 pints vegetable stock
100g/4oz vegetarian Parmesan-style
    cheese, grated
140g/5oz small pasta shapes
small bunch basil, shredded
crusty bread, to serve

1 Gently cook the onions, carrots and celery in the oil in a large pan for 20 minutes until soft. Splash in some water if they stick. Add the sugar, garlic, purée, herbs and courgettes, and cook for 4–5 minutes on a medium heat until they brown a little.

2 Pour in the beans, tomatoes and stock, then simmer for 20 minutes. Add half the cheese and the pasta, and simmer for 6–8 minutes until the pasta is cooked. Sprinkle with basil and the remaining cheese, and serve with hunks of crusty bread.

PER SERVING 215 kcals, protein 11g, carbs 30g, fat 6g, sat fat 3g, fibre 5g, sugar 12g, salt 1.06g

Pea & mint soup with cheese biscuits

For best results always liquidise the soup while it's still hot. If it is slightly too thick, adjust by adding extra stock. The cheese biscuits are delicate but utterly delicious.

TAKES 45 MINUTES • SERVES 6

1 tbsp olive oil
knob of butter
½ bunch spring onions, sliced, plus
  a few extra to garnish
1 potato, cut into small dice
1 litre/1¾ pints hot vegetable stock
900g/2lb frozen petits pois
½ small bunch mint, leaves picked,
  plus a few extra to garnish
85g/3oz vegetarian Parmesan-style
  cheese, very finely grated

1 Heat the oil and butter in a heavy-based pan. When foaming, add the onions and potato. Gently fry without colouring for about 5 minutes. Stir in the stock, bring to the boil and simmer for 10 minutes or until the potato is tender.
2 Stir in the peas, bring to the boil, then cook for about 3 minutes until they are just done. Remove the pan from the heat, add the mint leaves and whizz in a blender or food processor until smooth.
3 To make the biscuits, heat the grill to high. Line a baking sheet with baking parchment and divide the grated cheese into six long strips. Grill for 1 minute or until the cheese has melted and is lightly golden. While still warm and a bit flexible, lift biscuits from the parchment with a palette knife, then cool until firm.
4 To serve, heat the soup and divide among six bowls. Scatter with mint and onions, and serve with the biscuits.

PER SERVING 213 kcals, protein 15g, carbs 20g, fat 9g, sat fat 4g, fibre 8g, sugar 8g, salt 0.72g

Thai pumpkin soup

Make the most of the autumn abundance of squash and pumpkins. The Thai curry paste adds a kick to this soup, making it a warm and welcoming lunch.

TAKES 1 HOUR 5 MINUTES ● SERVES 6

1.5kg/3lb 5oz pumpkin or squash, peeled, deseeded and roughly chopped
4 tsp sunflower oil
1 onion, sliced
1 tbsp grated ginger
1 lemongrass stalk, bashed a little
3–4 tbsp Thai red curry paste
400ml can coconut milk
850ml/1½ pints vegetable stock
lime juice and sugar, to season (optional)
1 red chilli, deseeded and sliced, to garnish (optional)

1 Heat oven to 200C/180C fan/gas 6. Toss the pumpkin or squash in a roasting tin with half the oil and some seasoning, then roast for 30 minutes until the chunks are golden and tender.

2 Meanwhile, put the remaining oil in a pan with the onion, ginger and lemongrass. Gently cook for 8–10 minutes until softened. Stir in the curry paste for 1 minute, followed by the roasted pumpkin, all but 3 tablespoons of the coconut milk and the stock. Bring to a simmer, cook for 5 minutes, then fish out the lemongrass. Cool for a few minutes, then whizz the soup until smooth with a hand blender, or in a large blender in batches.

3 Return to the pan to heat through, seasoning with salt, pepper, lime juice and sugar, to taste. Serve drizzled with the remaining coconut milk and scattered with chilli, if you like.

PER SERVING 192 kcals, protein 4g, carbs 11g, fat 15g, sat fat 10g, fibre 4g, sugar 9g, salt 0.94g

Thai coconut & veg broth

Many curry pastes contain dried shrimp and fish sauce, so always read the labels carefully to make sure you're buying a vegetarian version.

TAKES 25 MINUTES • SERVES 4

1½ tbsp Thai red curry paste
1 tsp vegetable oil
1 litre/1¾ pints vegetable stock
400ml can half-fat coconut milk
2 tsp brown sugar
175g/6oz medium egg noodles
2 carrots, cut into matchsticks
½ head Chinese leaf, sliced
½ × 300g bag beansprouts
6 cherry tomatoes, halved
juice 1 lime
3 spring onions, halved, then finely sliced lengthways
handful of coriander, roughly chopped

1 Put the curry paste in a large pan or wok with the oil. Fry for 1 minute until fragrant. Tip in the vegetable stock, coconut milk and brown sugar. Simmer for 3 minutes.

2 Add the noodles, carrots and Chinese leaf, and simmer for 4–6 minutes, until everything is tender. Mix in the beansprouts and tomatoes. Add lime juice to taste and some extra seasoning, if you like. Spoon the soup into four bowls and sprinkle with sliced spring onions and coriander.

PER SERVING 338 kcals, protein 10g, carbs 46g, fat 14g, sat fat 7g, fibre 5g, sugar 12g, salt 1.19g

Spicy lentil soup with curry pinwheel rolls

Warming and satisfying, this soup is just right for chilly days. For a flavour change, replace the carrots with 3 medium parsnips.

TAKES 45 MINUTES ● **SERVES 4**

2 tbsp curry paste
1 onion, chopped
2 carrots, grated
140g/5oz red split lentils
1 litre/1¾ pints hot vegetable stock

FOR THE CURRY PINWHEEL ROLLS

500g pack bread mix
1 tbsp curry paste

1 Heat oven to 220C/200C fan/gas 7. For the rolls, make up the bread mix following the pack instructions, then roll out to a 30 × 40cm/12 × 16in rectangle. Spread over the curry paste, then roll up, starting with the longest edge, like a roly-poly. Cut into eight slices and transfer to a lightly oiled baking sheet. Bake for 20–25 minutes or until golden and cooked through.

2 Meanwhile, make the soup. Fry the curry paste and onion in a large pan for 2 minutes until fragrant. Stir in the carrots and lentils, and mix to coat in the curry paste. Cook for 2 minutes, then pour in the stock and simmer for 20 minutes until the lentils are tender. Whizz with a stick blender until smooth, add some seasoning and serve with the curry pinwheels.

PER SERVING 535 kcals, protein 23g, carbs 99g, fat 8g, sat fat 10g, fibre 11g, sugar 11g, salt 3.96g

Chunky root-vegetable soup with pesto toasts

A great soup to come home to on a winter's day. If you prefer a smoother soup, simply whizz in a blender and then reheat.

TAKES 55 MINUTES • SERVES 4

25g/1oz butter
2 shallots, finely chopped
2 garlic cloves, crushed
100ml/3½fl oz white wine
1 medium leek, chopped
1 medium parsnip, diced
1 large carrot, diced
1 swede, diced
1 litre/1¾ pints vegetable stock
100g/4oz mature Cheddar, grated
1 ciabatta loaf or small baguette, cut
   into 8 thin slices

FOR THE PESTO

25g pack flat-leaf parsley, finely
   chopped
25g pack chives, finely snipped
25g/1oz vegetarian Parmesan-style
   cheese, finely grated
2 garlic cloves, crushed
1 tbsp toasted pine nuts, chopped
olive oil

1 Melt the butter in a large heavy-based pan. Add the shallots and cook for 5 minutes until soft, then add the garlic and cook for 1 minute more. Pour in the wine and simmer until reduced, then add the vegetables and cook for 2–3 minutes.

2 Pour in the stock, bring to the boil, reduce the heat and simmer for about 20 minutes until the vegetables are soft.

3 Meanwhile, to make the pesto, mix all the ingredients together with enough olive oil to make a thickish paste. Season.

4 To make the toasts, put the grated cheese in a bowl and mix together with 2–3 teaspoons of the pesto. Heat the grill. Put the ciabatta or baguette slices under the grill and toast on both sides. Remove, top with the pesto–cheese mixture, then grill until melted.

5 Season the soup well and serve with the cheesy pesto toasts and any remaining pesto for drizzling.

PER SERVING 388 kcals, protein 15g, carbs 43g, fat 18g, sat fat 9g, fibre 9g, sugar 18g, salt 1.85g

Red lentil & sweet potato pâté

This low-fat pâté is a great idea to keep in the fridge for a home-from-school snack or to pack into a lunchbox with some crispy veg sticks.

TAKES 40 MINUTES ● SERVES 4

1 tbsp olive oil, plus extra for drizzling
½ onion, finely chopped
1 tsp smoked paprika, plus a little extra
1 small sweet potato, peeled and diced
140g/5oz red split lentils
3 thyme sprigs, leaves chopped, plus
   a few extra to garnish (optional)
500ml/18fl oz low-sodium vegetable
   stock
1 tsp red wine vinegar
pitta bread and vegetable sticks,
   to serve

1 Heat the oil in a large pan, add the onion and cook slowly until soft and golden. Tip in the paprika and cook for a further 2 minutes, then add the sweet potato, lentils, thyme and stock. Bring to a simmer, then cook for 20 minutes or until the potato and lentils are tender.

2 Add the vinegar and some seasoning, and roughly mash the mixture until you get a texture you like. Chill for 1 hour, then drizzle with the extra olive oil, dust with the extra paprika and sprinkle with thyme sprigs, if you like. Serve with pitta bread and vegetable sticks.

PER SERVING 200 kcals, protein 9g, carbs 28g, fat 5g, sat fat 1g, fibre 3g, sugar 5g, salt 0.4g

Black bean tostadas with avocado salsa

Corn tortillas are full of flavour, last for ages and make a nice change from flour tortillas. Look for them in the Mexican-food section of your supermarket.

TAKES 25 MINUTES • SERVES 4

8 corn tortillas
2 tbsp olive oil
1 onion, chopped
3 garlic cloves, chopped
1 tbsp smoked paprika
1 tbsp ground cumin
5 tbsp cider vinegar
3 tbsp clear honey
3 × 400g cans black beans, rinsed and drained
a few toppings – choose from chopped tomatoes, sliced red onion, diced avocado, sliced jalapeño peppers, coriander sprigs
crème fraîche or Tabasco chipotle sauce, to serve

1 Heat oven to 200C/180C fan/gas 6. Brush the tortillas with a little of the oil and place in a single layer on baking sheets. Cook for 8 minutes until crisp.
2 In a large frying pan, heat the remaining oil. Add the onion and garlic, and cook for 5 minutes. Add the spices, vinegar and honey. Cook for 2 minutes more. Add the beans and some seasoning, and heat through.
3 Remove from the heat and mash the beans gently with the back of a spoon to a chunky purée. Spread some beans over the crispy corn tortillas, scatter with your choice of toppings and add a spoonful of crème fraîche to cool down, or a splash of chipotle Tabasco to spice it up.

PER SERVING 675 kcals, protein 27g, carbs 91g, fat 17g, sat fat 7g, fibre 15g, sugar 18g, salt 0.6g

Pumpkin falafel pockets

These tasty little patties are good served with the carrot and feta salad in pitta bread for a moneywise lunch. Up the amount of chilli if you like things spicy.

TAKES 50 MINUTES, PLUS CHILLING

- **MAKES 4**

1kg/2lb 4oz pumpkin or butternut squash, deseeded and cut into wedges

400g can chickpeas, drained, rinsed and dried

1 garlic clove, chopped

½ tsp chilli flakes

1 tsp ground cumin

small bunch parsley, roughly chopped

2 slices white bread, whizzed to crumbs

4 wholemeal pitta breads, to serve

FOR THE SALAD

2 carrots, coarsely grated

½ small red onion, finely sliced

100g/4oz feta, crumbled

1 Put the pumpkin or squash in a microwave-safe bowl and cover with cling film. Cook on high for 10 minutes or until soft.

2 Tip the chickpeas, garlic, chilli flakes, cumin and half the parsley into a food processor, then whizz until the chickpeas are finely chopped but not smooth.

3 Allow the pumpkin or squash to cool slightly, then scoop the flesh from the skin and add to the chickpea mix with some seasoning and the breadcrumbs. Give everything a good stir, then shape into 12 little patties with your hands. Put the falafels on a plate and chill for 10 minutes.

4 Meanwhile, mix the remaining parsley with the grated carrot, onion and cheese, then set aside. Heat the grill to medium, then cook the falafels on a baking sheet for 3–5 minutes on each side. Split the pitta breads lengthways and fill with the warm falafels and some of the feta salad.

PER SERVING 346 kcals, protein 17g, carbs 54g, fat 8g, sat fat 4g, fibre 9g, sugar 9g, salt 1.91g

Chargrilled veg houmous with dippers

Hitting your 5-a-day target may seem tricky, but this tasty no-cook dip packs in three portions at one lunchtime sitting. Good for a home-from-school snack for the kids.

TAKES 10 MINUTES • SERVES 4

350g/12oz frozen chargrilled
   vegetables, defrosted
400g can chickpeas, rinsed and drained
1 garlic clove, chopped
juice ½ lemon
1 tsp olive oil

TO SERVE

2 wholemeal pitta breads, toasted and
   sliced
100g/4oz radishes, scrubbed
2 carrots, cut into batons
3 celery sticks, cut into batons

1 Tip the vegetables, most of the chickpeas, the garlic and lemon juice into the bowl of a food processor with some seasoning, then whizz until smooth.

2 Put the houmous into a serving bowl. Scatter over the reserved chickpeas and drizzle with the olive oil. Serve with toasted pitta slices and the vegetables to dip in.

PER SERVING 266 kcals, protein 12g,
carbs 40.3g, fat 5.9g, sat fat 0.8g, fibre 9.1g,
sugar 8.6g, salt 0.4g

Squash, goat's cheese & rosemary pancakes

Sweet or savoury, pancakes are always a big hit with all the family, especially the kids. These pancakes make a great light lunch or brunch dish.

TAKES 40 MINUTES • MAKES ABOUT 8

200g/7oz self-raising flour
1 tsp baking powder
1 rosemary sprig, leaves finely chopped
1 egg
300ml/½ pint milk
25g/1oz butter, melted and cooled, plus
   a knob extra for frying
2 tbsp olive oil
250g/9oz butternut squash, peeled,
   deseeded and cut into small cubes
100g/4oz goat's cheese, crumbled into
   small pieces
dressed rocket leaf salad, handful
   pumpkin seeds and onion chutney,
   to serve

1 Mix the flour, baking powder, rosemary and a good pinch of salt in a large bowl. Beat the egg with the milk. Make a well in the centre of the dry ingredients and whisk in the milk mixture and melted butter to make a thick, smooth batter. Put in the fridge while you prepare the rest of the ingredients.

2 Over a medium heat, add a knob of butter and 1 teaspoon oil to a large pan, then add the squash and cook for 10 minutes until tender, turning up the heat for the final few minutes to brown a little. Remove the batter from the fridge, add the goat's cheese and squash, then carefully fold everything together.

3 Heat a little oil in a non-stick frying pan, then, in batches, add a ladleful of batter per pancake. Allow to cook for 3 minutes until bubbles cover the surface, then flip over and cook the other side until golden. Serve with dressed rocket salad, a few pumpkin seeds and onion chutney.

PER SERVING 269 kcals, protein 10g, carbs 29g, fat 13g, sat fat 7g, fibre 2g, sugar 5g, salt 0.9g

Crostini with pea purée, rocket & broad beans

A perfect seasonal starter for summer meals, or serve the pea purée as a delicious dip in a small bowl with toasted ciabatta alongside.

TAKES 25 MINUTES • SERVES 6

200g/7oz double-podded broad beans
400g/14oz frozen peas
85g/3oz butter
leaves from small bunch mint
100g/4oz natural yogurt
1 small bunch dill, chopped
1 ciabatta loaf, sliced
couple of handfuls rocket leaves
140g/5oz radishes, thinly sliced
85g/3oz pecorino cheese
extra virgin olive oil, for drizzling
   (optional)

1 Cook the broad beans in a pan of boiling water for 4 minutes until just tender. Drain, cool under cold running water, then drain again and set aside. In the same pan, fry the peas in half the butter until just cooked. Allow to cool, then blitz with a hand blender or in a food processor with the mint, yogurt and some seasoning until smooth.
2 Heat oven to 180C/160C fan/gas 4. Melt the rest of the butter in a small pan, stir in the dill, then brush over the slices of bread. Bake for 10–12 minutes until the bread is crisp and golden.
3 Spread some pea purée on to each slice, then top with rocket, broad beans and radishes. Use a potato peeler to shave the cheese on top. Drizzle with olive oil, if you like, before serving.

PER SERVING 383 kcals, protein 16g, carbs 37g, fat 20g, sat fat 11g, fibre 7g, sugar 6g, salt 1.95g

Tofu & vegetable patties

These versatile patties could be made bite-sized to serve as tempting canapés or just a little smaller for children to enjoy them in a burger bun with some tomato ketchup.

TAKES 25 MINUTES • MAKES 8

1 carrot, grated
bunch spring onions, sliced, plus extra
    strips to garnish (optional)
1 garlic clove, crushed
3cm/1¼in piece ginger, grated
400g block firm tofu, drained and
    crumbled
2 eggs, lightly beaten
2 tbsp each sesame and vegetable oil
sweet chilli sauce, to serve (optional)

1 Combine all the ingredients except the oils in a large bowl with some seasoning and mix well. Heat both the oils in a frying pan. Grease an 8cm metal pastry ring or cookie cutter and place in the pan. When hot, pour in 5 tablespoons of the tofu batter and turn down the heat to medium.

2 Cook for 4–5 minutes until golden, then take off the ring (be careful, as it may be hot), flip the patty and cook the other side. Do this in batches, keeping the finished patties warm in a low oven. Serve with the chilli sauce and garnish with extra spring onions, if you like.

PER SERVING 110 kcals, protein 6g, carbs 3g, fat 9g, sat fat 1g, fibre 1g, sugar 1g, salt 0.11g

Garlic mushrooms on toast

These creamy mushrooms make a quick and tempting lunch on toasted baguettes. The mushrooms are also good served with pasta bows.

TAKES 15 MINUTES • SERVES 4

2 tsp vegetable oil
500g pack mushrooms, halved
2 garlic cloves, crushed
½ × 300g tub garlic and herb soft
   cheese
150ml/¼ pint hot vegetable stock
2 small baguettes, sliced open and
   halved

1 Heat the oil in a large frying pan, then tip in the mushrooms and garlic, and cook for 3 minutes. Stir in the soft cheese and the stock, and simmer for 2 minutes.

2 Lightly toast the baguettes, top with the warm mushroom mix and a grinding of black pepper, and serve.

PER SERVING 355 kcals, protein 11g, carbs 37g, fat 19g, sat fat 10g, fibre 3g, sugar 3g, salt 1.47g

Red onion & chilli bhajis with mint raita

You can pick up a bag of chickpea flour in health-food shops, Indian stores or supermarkets, where it is often called gram flour.

TAKES 40 MINUTES • MAKES 12

100g/4oz chickpea flour (gram flour)

½ tsp baking powder

2 tsp curry paste or powder

1 red or green chilli, deseeded and finely chopped

2 red onions, 1 finely chopped, 1 thinly sliced

vegetable oil, for frying

FOR THE RAITA

150g tub natural yogurt

2 tbsp chopped mint, plus a few extra leaves to garnish

1 small garlic clove, crushed

1 Sift the flour and baking powder into a bowl. Add the curry paste or powder, chopped chilli and a good sprinkling of salt. Add about 150ml/¼ pint cold water to make a thick batter. Stir in the chopped and sliced onions until they are well coated in the batter.

2 Mix together the raita ingredients with a little salt and pepper, then spoon into a small bowl.

3 Heat about 5cm/2in of oil in a wok or deep pan. Add a tiny speck of batter, if it rises to the surface surrounded by bubbles and starts to brown, then the oil is hot enough to start woking.

4 Add heaped tablespoons of onion mix to the pan, a few at a time, and cook for a few minutes, turning once, until they are evenly browned and crisp, about 3–4 minutes. Drain on kitchen paper, sprinkle with a little salt and keep warm while you cook the remaining bhajis. Serve with the raita.

PER SERVING 102 kcals, protein 3g, carbs 7g, fat 7g, sat fat 1g, fibre 1g, sugar 2g, salt 0.09g

Spinach samosas with Indian salad

These low-fat samosas can be served hot or cold and are brilliant for lunchboxes. Using frozen spinach cuts down on the cooking time.

TAKES 45 MINUTES ● **SERVES 4**

FOR THE SAMOSAS

600g/1lb 5oz frozen chopped spinach, defrosted and drained
4 spring onions, trimmed and sliced
100g/4oz cherry tomatoes, quartered
1 tbsp garam masala
6 sheets filo pastry
2 tbsp olive oil

FOR THE SALAD

100g/4oz cherry tomatoes, halved
4 spring onions, sliced
1 carrot, cut or peeled into long strips
1 tsp mustard seeds
1 green chilli, sliced
juice ½ lime

1 Heat oven to 200C/180C fan/gas 6. In a large bowl, mix the spinach, spring onions, cherry tomatoes and garam masala with a grinding of pepper.

2 Lay out a sheet of filo and cut it lengthways into three long strips. Brush roughly with the oil – don't worry about covering the whole sheet. Spoon tablespoons of mix on to the top of each strip and fold each over into a triangle. Keep folding until each strip of filo is used up. Repeat with the other filo sheets. Brush the samosas with any remaining oil, then bake for 20 minutes until golden and crisp.

3 To make the salad, toss all the ingredients together and serve alongside the samosas.

PER SERVING 224 kcals, protein 9g, carbs 28g, fat 9g, sat fat 1g, fibre 6g, sugar 9g, salt 0.85g

Tex-Mex burrito

Filled with cheesy scrambled eggs, these wraps make a great quick lunch. If you've bought a pack of wraps, cover the leftovers in cling film and freeze for another time.

TAKES 20 MINUTES • SERVES 2

2 tomatoes, halved, seeds scooped
   out, then sliced
3 spring onions, chopped
1 red chilli, sliced (deseeded, if you like
   it milder)
4 eggs
100ml/3½fl oz milk
1 tsp olive oil
100g/4oz Cheddar, grated
2 large wraps
soured cream and guacamole,
   to serve

1 In a small bowl, mix the tomatoes, half the spring onions and half the red chilli with some seasoning and set aside. Beat together the eggs and milk with a fork with some seasoning.

2 Heat the oil in a large non-stick pan and fry the remaining spring onions and chilli for 1 minute, then pour in the egg mix. Gently scramble the eggs by dragging the egg mixture as it sets into the middle of the pan. Cook to your liking, then take off the heat and throw on the cheese. Stir through, then divide between the wraps. Tuck up the top and bottom of each wrap and roll up, then slice in half and serve with the homemade tomato salsa, soured cream and some guacamole.

PER SERVING 611 kcals, protein 35g, carbs 33g, fat 38g, sat fat 16g, fibre 2g, sugar 6g, salt 1.96g

Spicy vegetable egg-fried rice

This moneywise meal is a good way of using up leftover rice. Use your favourite veg –
broccoli, pak choy, baby corn and mangetout are all great additions.

TAKES 30 MINUTES • SERVES 4

200g/7oz basmati rice or 400g/14oz
  leftover cooked rice
1–2 red chillies, deseeded and very
  finely chopped
3 garlic cloves, crushed
1 tbsp sunflower oil
2 large carrots, diced
200g/7oz Chinese cabbage, finely
  sliced
2 eggs, lightly beaten
3 spring onions, sliced
200g/7oz frozen peas
1 tbsp soy sauce, plus extra for serving
  (optional)

1 If making the rice fresh, cook it according to the pack instructions, then drain. Blend the chillies and garlic (in a pestle and mortar, if you have one) with a pinch of salt, to make a paste.

2 Heat the oil in a wok or large frying pan on a medium–high heat. Add the carrots and stir-fry for 5 minutes until tender. Add the cabbage and chilli paste, and cook for 1 minute more. Tip in the cooked basmati or leftover rice and stir-fry for 1 minute until piping hot.

3 Push the rice mixture to one side of the pan. Add the eggs to the cleared space and scramble until set. Mix in the onions, peas and soy, and stir-fry everything together until the peas are hot. Serve straight away with extra soy sauce, if you like.

PER SERVING 305 kcals, protein 12g, carbs 52g, fat 7g, sat fat 2g, fibre 6g, sugar 8g, salt 0.84g

Halloumi with chickpea & couscous salsa

A chewy white cheese originating from Cyprus, halloumi has a mild salty flavour. It lends itself well to cooking because of its firm texture, which is retained when cooked.

TAKES 20 MINUTES • **SERVES 4**

250g/9oz couscous
250ml/9fl oz hot vegetable stock
400g can chickpeas, rinsed and drained
140g/5oz cherry tomatoes, halved
3 tbsp olive oil
3 tbsp sherry vinegar or red wine vinegar
1 red chilli, ½ deseeded and finely chopped, ½ sliced
small bunch each mint and coriander leaves, chopped
250g pack halloumi, thickly sliced

1 Put the couscous in a bowl and pour over the hot stock. Cover with cling film, leave to stand and swell for 10 minutes.
2 Make the salsa by mixing the chickpeas with the tomatoes, half the oil and vinegar, the finely chopped chilli and some of the chopped herbs. Season and arrange among four serving plates.
3 Heat a griddle pan or frying pan. Fry the halloumi for 2–3 minutes on each side, until golden and lightly charred.
4 Fluff up the couscous with a fork and mix in the rest of the oil, vinegar and herbs with some seasoning. Pile on to the plates next to the salsa and top with the warm halloumi. Garnish with the sliced chilli.

PER SERVING 489 kcals, protein 21g, carbs 44g, fat 27g, sat fat 11g, fibre 3g, sugar 3g, salt 2.79g

Paneer with broccoli & sesame

Asafoetida is a pungent powdered spice used in Indian cooking. It has a very powerful onion flavour so should always be used sparingly.

TAKES 25 MINUTES ● SERVES 4

200g/7oz sprouting broccoli
1 tbsp vegetable oil
pinch asafoetida
1 tsp cumin seeds
1 tbsp sesame seeds
1 large green chilli, finely chopped
½ tsp brown mustard seeds
6 curry leaves
1 medium onion, sliced
140g/5oz paneer cheese, cut into strips
1 tbsp grated ginger
2 garlic cloves, crushed
1 tsp lemon juice
½ tsp ground mace

1 Trim the broccoli and boil or steam for 5–6 minutes until tender but firm to the bite. Drain and cool under cold running water.

2 Heat the oil in a wok or large frying pan, then add the asafoetida, cumin seeds, sesame seeds, chilli, mustard seeds and curry leaves. Cook for 1 minute until fragrant, then add the onion and cook for another 2 minutes.

3 Throw in the paneer, ginger and garlic, and season. Cook on a medium heat for 4–5 minutes until the paneer turns golden. Add the broccoli and mix through the paneer and spices, then add lemon juice, mace and a twist of pepper. Serve with steamed rice.

PER SERVING 195 kcals, protein 11g, carbs 5g, fat 14g, sat fat 6g, fibre 3g, sugar 3g, salt 1.3g

Creamy tagliatelle with fennel

Cooking the sliced fennel gives it a mellow, subtle flavour, and the fennel seeds add an interesting crunch to this new-style lemony pasta dish.

TAKES 25 MINUTES • SERVES 4

1 tbsp olive oil
2 fennel bulbs, halved and thinly sliced
2 tsp fennel seeds
3 garlic cloves, finely chopped
300g/10oz tagliatelle or fettuccine
large pinch lemon zest and a squeeze
   of juice
6 tbsp mascarpone
handful flat-leaf parsley, roughly
   chopped

1 Add the oil to a non-stick frying pan. Tip in the sliced fennel and cook for 10 minutes until soft and slightly golden, adding the fennel seeds and garlic for the final 3 minutes of cooking.

2 Meanwhile, cook the pasta according to the pack instructions, reserving a few tablespoons of the cooking water to add to the sauce.

3 Stir the lemon zest, juice, mascarpone and most of the parsley into the fennel mixture. Heat through then toss in the cooked pasta and a few tablespoons of the cooking water. Give everything a good stir and season. Scatter over the remaining parsley and serve.

PER SERVING 403 kcals, protein 11g, carbs 62g, fat 14g, sat fat 7g, fibre 4g, sugar 3g, salt 0.09g

Gnocchi with courgette & mascarpone

The freshness of the lemon, combined with the warmth of the chilli and the creamy sauce make this a wonderful dish for a laid-back summer lunch.

TAKES 20 MINUTES • SERVES 2

300g/10oz fresh gnocchi
1 tbsp olive oil
1 red chilli, sliced (deseeded, if you like)
1 medium courgette, cut into thin
    ribbons with a peeler
4 spring onions, chopped
zest 1 lemon
2 heaped tbsp mascarpone
50g/2oz vegetarian Parmesan-style
    cheese, grated
dressed mixed salad leaves, to serve

1 Cook the gnocchi according to the pack instructions. Drain, reserving a ladle of the cooking water, and set aside.
2 Heat the oil in a frying pan. Cook the chilli and courgette for 3 minutes until soft. Add the spring onions, lemon zest, mascarpone, half the cheese and the reserved cooking water. Mix until smooth, add the cooked gnocchi and heat through.
3 Season, divide between two ovenproof dishes and scatter with the remaining cheese. Grill for 2–3 minutes until bubbling and serve with the dressed mixed leaves.

PER SERVING 498 kcals, protein 17g, carbs 54g, fat 25g, sat fat 13g, fibre 3g, sugar 6g, salt 2.07g

Portobello & blue cheese melts

These flavoursome mushrooms topped with melted blue cheese taste terrific as a vegetarian burger. Good for lunch for one or make more to serve a crowd.

TAKES 25 MINUTES ● MAKES 1

1 red onion, cut into wedges
1 tsp olive oil
2 tbsp balsamic vinegar
2 Portobello or flat mushrooms
1 tsp thyme leaves
25g/1oz blue cheese
1 ciabatta bread roll
handful rocket leaves
oven fries and tomato ketchup,
   to serve (optional)

1 Heat oven to 220C/200C fan/gas 7. Mix the onion with the oil and vinegar, spread on a baking sheet, then put the mushrooms on top, stem-side up, and scatter over the thyme and some seasoning. Cook in the oven for 15 minutes, until the onions start to soften and caramelise.

2 Crumble the blue cheese into the cavity of the mushrooms and cook for 5 minutes more until the cheese is melted and bubbling.

3 Split the ciabatta roll in half and lightly toast. Pile the bottom half with a handful of rocket, the sticky onions and the cheese-topped mushrooms, and top with the other half of the roll. Serve with oven fries, if you like.

PER MELT 444 kcals, protein 20g, carbs 59g, fat 16g, sat fat 6g, fibre 6g, sugar 12g, salt 2.34g

Creamy lemon & cabbage pasta

The crispy, chunky crumbs add an interesting texture to this lemony pasta dish.
Use your favourite pasta shape, such as penne, twists or farfalle.

TAKES 30 MINUTES • **SERVES 2**

2 large handfuls fresh chunky
  breadcrumbs
3 tbsp olive oil
3 garlic cloves, finely chopped
200g/7oz short pasta
1 medium onion, chopped
125ml/4fl oz white wine
zest ½ lemon
140g/5oz crème fraîche
½ small head Savoy cabbage, very
  thinly sliced

1 Heat oven to 200C/180C fan/gas 6. In a bowl, mix the breadcrumbs with half the oil and one of the garlic cloves, and season well. Spread out on a large baking sheet and bake for 8 minutes, until crisp and golden. Remove and set aside.

2 Cook the pasta in a large pan of boiling water until al dente. Meanwhile, pour the remaining oil into a frying pan, add the onion and remaining garlic, season and cook for about 4 minutes until golden, then add the wine and lemon zest. Reduce for a few minutes, then add the crème fraîche. Remove from the heat but keep warm.

3 Add the cabbage to the pasta water for the last 3 minutes of the cooking time. Drain and return to the pan, add the creamy sauce to the pasta and cabbage, and toss together. Divide between two bowls and top with the crumbs.

PER SERVING 963 kcals, protein 21g, carbs 114g, fat 48g, sat fat 21g, fibre 9g, sugar 16g, salt 0.68g

Stuffed sweet peppers

These peppers have a fabulous flavour when cooked on the barbecue. To increase the smoky taste, cook them with the barbecue lid on.

TAKES 30 MINUTES • SERVES 4

4 peppers, halved lengthways through
  the stalk and deseeded
1 tbsp extra virgin olive oil, plus extra
  to drizzle (optional)
2 × 125g balls mozzarella, sliced
2 tbsp black olives, chopped
1 tbsp chopped oregano
2 garlic cloves, crushed
crusty bread, to serve

1 Heat the barbecue or griddle pan to hot. Rub the outside of the peppers all over with the olive oil.

2 Stuff the peppers with the mozzarella, olives, oregano and garlic, and drizzle with a touch more olive oil, if you like.

3 Pop on the barbecue, stuffed-side up, for 12–15 minutes until the peppers are nicely charred (or roast in a baking tin in the oven at 220C/200C fan/gas 7 for the same amount of time). Serve straight away with some crusty bread.

PER SERVING 282 kcals, protein 13g, carbs 8g, fat 22g, sat fat 9g, fibre 2g, sugar 7g, salt 0.73g

Tomato & goat's cheese couscous

This dish makes a good light summer lunch or, even better, pack it up for a picnic. Crumbled blue cheese can be used instead of the goat's cheese.

TAKES 20 MINUTES • SERVES 4

200g/7oz couscous
200ml/7fl oz hot vegetable stock
4 large ripe tomatoes, halved
1 tbsp chopped oregano leaves
2 tbsp balsamic vinegar
200g/7oz firm goat's cheese, crumbled

1 Tip the couscous into a heatproof bowl and pour over the vegetable stock. Cover with cling film and set aside for 15 minutes.

2 Fluff the couscous with a fork then tear and squash the tomatoes into bite-sized pieces with your hands over the bowl of couscous, and stir in.

3 Add the oregano, balsamic and some seasoning, then crumble in the goat's cheese before you serve.

PER SERVING 328 kcals, protein 16g, carbs 32g, fat 16g, sat fat 9g, fibre 2g, sugar 6g, salt 1.04g

Spring vegetable tagliatelle with lemon sauce

This budget-beating pasta dish, topped with the new season's spring veg, looks and tastes good enough for a casual supper with friends.

TAKES 30 MINUTES • SERVES 4

450g/1lb mixed spring vegetables, such as green beans, asparagus, broad beans, peas
400g/14oz tagliatelle
1 lemon
1 tbsp Dijon mustard
1 tbsp olive oil
3 tbsp snipped chives
shaved vegetarian-style Parmesan cheese, to garnish

1 Halve the green beans and cut the asparagus into three pieces on the diagonal. Cook the tagliatelle, adding the vegetables for the final 5 minutes of the cooking time.

2 Meanwhile, grate the zest from half the lemon and squeeze the juice from the whole lemon. Put the juice in a small pan with the mustard, olive oil and a little black pepper. Warm through, stirring until smooth.

3 Drain the pasta and veg, adding 4 tablespoons of the cooking water to the lemon sauce. Return the pasta to the pan, reheat the sauce, adding most of the chives, then add to the pasta, tossing everything together well. Divide among four shallow bowls and top each with a grinding of black pepper, a few shavings of cheese and the remaining chives.

PER SERVING 469 kcals, protein 21g, carbs 84g, fat 8g, sat fat 3g, fibre 7g, sugar 4g, salt 0.48g

Artichoke & roasted pepper soufflé omelette

Omelettes are always a quick and easy supper to put together. Ring the changes with this light and fluffy omelette with its tasty filling.

TAKES 25 MINUTES • SERVES 4

5 eggs, separated, plus 2 whole eggs
½ can artichoke hearts, drained,
    quartered if whole
1 whole roasted pepper from a jar or
    can, drained, patted dry and roughly
    chopped
50g/2oz vegetarian Parmesan-style
    cheese, grated
10 large basil leaves, shredded
1 tbsp butter
1 tbsp extra virgin rapeseed or olive oil
rocket and baby leaf salad with a
    balsamic dressing, to serve

1 In a large bowl, lightly beat together the 5 egg yolks and 2 whole eggs. In a separate bowl, use an electric whisk to beat the egg whites until stiff. Add the whites to the beaten eggs and yolks, and fold together carefully, keeping the mixture light and fluffy. Fold in the artichokes, pepper, half the cheese, the basil, and some salt and pepper.

2 Heat grill to high. Heat a medium non-stick frying pan over a medium heat. Add the butter and oil. When the butter has melted, add the omelette mixture and spread it evenly over the base of the pan. Cook until golden underneath, about 5 minutes. Scatter over the remaining cheese, then put the pan under the grill and cook for a further 2 minutes.

3 Slide the omelette on to a board or serving plate. Cut into wedges and serve with a rocket and baby leaf salad with a balsamic dressing.

PER SERVING 275 kcals, protein 19g, carbs 2g, fat 21g, sat fat 8g, fibre 1g, sugar 1g, salt 1.01g

Spicy mushroom & broccoli noodles

Quick to prepare and cook, with a lovely fresh flavour, this stir-fry can easily be doubled to serve four. It makes a great warm-you-up supper on a chilly night.

TAKES 20 MINUTES • SERVES 2

1 low-salt vegetable stock cube
2 nests medium egg noodles
1 small head broccoli, broken into
    florets
1 tbsp sesame oil, plus extra to serve
    (optional)
250g pack shiitake or chestnut
    mushrooms, thickly sliced
1 fat garlic clove, finely chopped
½ tsp chilli flakes, or crumble 1 dried
    chilli into pieces
4 spring onions, thinly sliced
2 tbsp hoisin sauce
handful roasted cashew nuts, to serve

1 Put the stock cube into a pan of water, then bring to the boil. Add the noodles, bring the stock back to the boil and cook for 2 minutes. Add the broccoli and boil for 2 minutes more. Reserve a cup of the stock, then drain the noodles and veg.

2 Heat a frying pan or wok, add the sesame oil and stir-fry the mushrooms for 2 minutes until turning golden. Add the garlic, chilli flakes and most of the spring onions, cook for 1 minute more, then tip in the noodles and broccoli. Splash in 3 tablespoons of the stock and the hoisin sauce, then toss together for 1 minute using a pair of tongs or two wooden spoons.

3 Serve the noodles scattered with the cashew nuts and remaining spring onions. Add a dash more sesame oil to taste, if you like.

PER SERVING 624 kcals, protein 25g, carbs 105g, fat 14g, sat fat 2g, fibre 8g, sugar 17g, salt 2.35g

Creamy pea & watercress pasta

This recipe would be equally delicious made with the same quantity of shelled and podded broad beans instead of peas. You could also use mint instead of tarragon.

TAKES 25 MINUTES • SERVES 4

350g/12oz penne or other short pasta shape
300g/10oz fresh peas
1 garlic clove, peeled
100g bag watercress, tough stalks removed
2 tbsp mascarpone
2 tbsp chopped tarragon leaves
zest and juice 1 lemon
crusty bread, to serve

1 Cook the pasta according to the pack instructions. Meanwhile, cook the peas and garlic in a separate pan of boiling salted water for 3–5 minutes, until tender. Drain both well, keeping some of the pasta cooking water.

2 Put the peas, garlic and watercress in a food processor with 2 tablespoons of the pasta cooking water. Whizz to a very rough purée.

3 Return the pasta to the pan. Stir in the pea mixture, mascarpone, tarragon and lemon zest and juice. Season with some salt and pepper, and serve with crusty bread.

PER SERVING 410 kcals, protein 17g, carbs 76g, fat 7g, sat fat 3g, fibre 7g, sugar 4g, salt 0.08g

Spaghetti omelette

This is a tasty way of using up leftover cooked pasta. Don't fancy courgettes? Use 125g drained canned sweetcorn, or cooked and drained frozen sweetcorn instead.

TAKES 30 MINUTES • SERVES 4

2 tbsp olive oil
1 garlic clove, crushed
1 onion, chopped
2 courgettes, grated
2 tbsp chopped flat-leaf parsley
300g pot fresh cheese sauce
200g/7oz cooked spaghetti
2 eggs
green salad, to serve

1 Heat half the oil in a medium non-stick frying pan and add the garlic and onion. Cook for 2–3 minutes, until softened. Using your hands, squeeze out as much moisture from the courgettes as possible. Add them to the pan and cook for a further 3–4 minutes, until tender.

2 Spoon the vegetables into a large bowl. Stir in the parsley, cheese sauce and spaghetti, and season. Beat the eggs and stir into the mixture.

3 Heat the remaining oil in the frying pan and tip in the omelette mixture. Level it out with the back of a spoon and cook over a medium heat for 3–5 minutes, until almost set.

4 Heat the grill to high. Transfer the pan to the grill and cook for 2–3 minutes, until golden. Leave to cool in the pan for 5 minutes, then cut into wedges and serve with a green salad.

PER SERVING 324 kcals, protein 13g, carbs 21g, fat 22g, sat fat 8g, fibre 2g, sugar 5g, salt 0.68g

Spaghetti with spinach & walnut pesto

The fresh herbs add a wonderfully fragrant flavour to this low-fat pasta dish. If you like, substitute your favourite herbs – basil or tarragon would be good.

TAKES 30 MINUTES • SERVES 4

1 garlic clove, crushed
50g/2oz walnuts, roughly chopped
small bunch mint, roughly chopped
small bunch parsley, roughly chopped
zest and juice 1 lemon
350g/12oz wholewheat spaghetti
50g/2oz raisins
100g bag baby leaf spinach
extra virgin olive oil, to drizzle (optional)

1 Make the pesto by whizzing the garlic, walnuts, herbs, lemon zest and juice with some seasoning in a food processor until finely chopped.

2 Cook the spaghetti according to the pack instructions, then drain, reserving a little of the cooking water. Return to the pan and stir in the pesto, raisins and spinach with a splash of the cooking water. Serve with a drizzle of extra virgin olive oil, if you like.

PER SERVING 414 kcals, protein 15g, carbs 68g, fat 11g, sat fat 1g, fibre 9g, sugar 13g, salt 0.40g

Gnocchi with lemon & chive pesto

Gnocchi makes a welcome change from pasta in this authentic-tasting dish. Increase the veg count by including some small broccoli florets, green beans or peas.

TAKES 15 MINUTES ● SERVES 2

1 garlic clove, finely chopped
small bunch parsley, finely chopped
small bunch chives, snipped
2 tbsp toasted pine nuts, roughly
    chopped
2 tbsp grated vegetarian Parmesan-
    style cheese, plus extra for serving
    (optional)
zest and juice 1 lemon
4 tbsp olive oil
500g pack gnocchi

1 Put the garlic, herbs, pine nuts, cheese and lemon zest in a small bowl, season well, then stir in the lemon juice and olive oil. Set aside.

2 Cook the gnocchi in a pan of salted boiling water according to the pack instructions, then drain well. Tip into a serving bowl and toss through the pesto. Serve with extra grated cheese, if you like.

PER SERVING 667 kcals, protein 15g, carbs 85g, fat 32g, sat fat 6g, fibre 4g, sugar 5g, salt 2.7g

Quinoa with stir-fried winter veg

Quinoa is protein-rich, low-fat, gluten-free and makes a nutritious change from rice or pasta. This healthy dish counts as three of your 5-a-day.

TAKES 30 MINUTES • SERVES 4

200g/7oz quinoa
5 tbsp olive oil
2 garlic cloves, finely chopped
3 carrots, cut into thin sticks
300g/10oz leeks, sliced
300g/10oz broccoli, cut into small
    florets
100g/4oz sun-dried tomatoes, drained
    and chopped
200ml/7fl oz vegetable stock
2 tsp tomato purée
juice 1 lemon

1 Cook the quinoa according to the pack instructions. Meanwhile, heat 3 tablespoons of the oil in a wok or large pan, then add the garlic and quickly fry for 1 minute. Throw in the carrots, leeks and broccoli, then stir-fry for 2 minutes until everything is glistening.

2 Add the sun-dried tomatoes. Mix together the stock and tomato purée, then add to the pan. Cover, then cook for 3 minutes. Drain the quinoa, then toss in the remaining oil and the lemon juice. Divide the quinoa among warm plates and spoon the vegetables on top.

PER SERVING 414 kcals, protein 15g, carbs 42g, fat 22g, sat fat 3g, fibre 9g, sugar 14g, salt 1.03g

Spiced chickpea & potato fry-up

This mildly spiced chickpea dish is cooked in one pot and is really easy to make. If you're a spice lover, add hot chilli powder to taste.

TAKES 30 MINUTES • SERVES 4

300g/10oz potatoes, cut into small
   pieces
2 onions, sliced
2 garlic cloves, crushed
1 tsp olive oil
1 tsp each ground coriander, turmeric
   and mild chilli powder
1 tbsp cumin seeds
410g can chickpeas, rinsed and drained
2 tbsp tomato purée
200g/7oz baby leaf spinach
small bunch coriander, leaves chopped
wholemeal chapatis, low-fat natural
   yogurt and mango chutney, to serve

1 Boil the potatoes in salted water until just tender. While they are cooking, soften the onions and garlic in the oil in a frying pan for a few minutes. Add all the spices, then fry for 1 minute more. Stir in the chickpeas and tomato purée with 400ml/14fl oz water, then turn the heat up and bubble for a few minutes.

2 When the potatoes are ready, drain and add to the pan. Cook for a few minutes until the sauce is thick, stir in the spinach, then season. When the spinach has wilted, scatter with coriander and serve with the chapatis, yogurt and chutney on the side.

PER SERVING 201 kcals, protein 10g, carbs 33g, fat 4g, sat fat none, fibre 6g, sugar 6g, salt 0.66g

Warm quinoa salad with grilled halloumi

Quinoa is brilliant for vegetarians as it contains good levels of protein. It is gluten-free and an excellent source of calcium, iron and B vitamins.

TAKES 40 MINUTES • SERVES 3

3 tbsp extra virgin olive oil
1 small red onion, sliced
1 large roasted pepper from a jar, thickly sliced, or a handful ready-roasted sliced peppers
200g/7oz quinoa
500ml/18fl oz vegetable stock
small bunch flat-leaf parsley, roughly chopped
zest and juice 1 lemon
large pinch sugar
250g pack halloumi, cut into 6 slices

1 Heat 1 tablespoon of the oil in a medium pan. Cook the onion and pepper for a few minutes, then add the quinoa and cook for a further 3 minutes. Add the stock, cover and turn the heat down to a simmer. Cook for 15 minutes or until soft, then stir through half the parsley. Heat the grill.

2 Meanwhile, mix the lemon zest and juice with the remaining parsley and oil, and a large pinch of sugar and salt to make a dressing. Grill the halloumi slices until both sides are golden and crisp. Serve the warm salad with the grilled halloumi and the dressing poured over everything.

PER SERVING 603 kcals, protein 28g, carbs 40g, fat 37g, sat fat 16g, fibre 1g, sugar 7g, salt 3.1g

Preserved lemon & tomato salad with feta

Light and crunchy, tart and fruity, this simple Moroccan salad is deliciously refreshing served on its own with fresh, warm crusty bread, or as part of a vegetarian spread.

TAKES 15 MINUTES • SERVES 4

4 large tomatoes, deseeded and cut into thick strips
1 large red onion, thinly sliced
1 preserved lemon, pulp removed and rind cut into thin strips, or grated zest 1 lemon
200g pack feta
2 tbsp olive oil
juice ½ lemon
small bunch each flat-leaf parsley and mint, finely shredded

1 Put the tomatoes, onion and lemon rind or zest in a shallow bowl or on a platter. Crumble the feta over, drizzle with oil and lemon juice, and scatter over the parsley and mint.
2 Toss gently just before serving.

PER SERVING 215 kcals, protein 10g, carbs 9g, fat 16g, sat fat 7g, fibre 2g, sugar 7g, salt 1.49g

Orange, walnut & blue cheese salad

Crunchy, fruity, zingy and on the table in 15 minutes – this recipe ticks all the boxes for a refreshing supper, just add some hunks of crusty bread.

TAKES 15 MINUTES • SERVES 4

2 × 100g bags rocket, watercress and spinach salad

2 oranges

1 tbsp walnut oil

85g/3oz walnut pieces, roughly chopped

140g/5oz blue cheese, crumbled

1 Empty the bags of salad into a large bowl. Peel the oranges over a small bowl to catch the juices; then, over the same bowl, cut the segments from the pith and reserve.

2 Whisk the walnut oil into the orange juice, season, and pour over the salad leaves. Toss the salad, then arrange on a large platter. Scatter over the orange segments, walnuts and blue cheese.

PER SERVING 356 kcals, protein 14g, carbs 8g, fat 30g, sat fat 10g, fibre 3g, sugar 8g, salt 0.8g

Layered salad with cheese croutons

This layered salad is perfect for a picnic as it can be transported in its layers in a large covered container and then tossed just before serving.

TAKES 40 MINUTES • SERVES 6

3 thick slices white bread (day-old is better)
1 tbsp olive oil, plus extra for greasing
75g/2½oz vegetarian Parmesan-style cheese, 25g grated, 50g shaved
500g/1lb 2oz new potatoes, thickly sliced
200g/7oz green beans
4 Baby Gem lettuces, leaves separated and torn

FOR THE DRESSING

150g pot fat-free natural yogurt
25g/1oz vegetarian Parmesan-style cheese, finely grated
juice ½–1 lemon, depending on taste
2–3 tbsp olive oil
2 tbsp white wine vinegar
dash Tabasco sauce
1 garlic clove, crushed

1 Heat oven to 220C/200C fan/gas 7. Cut the bread into bite-sized chunks and toss with the olive oil and some seasoning. Put on to a well-oiled baking sheet and sprinkle the grated cheese over the bread. Cook for 10–12 minutes until golden and crisp. Remove and cool.

2 Cook the potatoes in a large pan of boiling water for about 8 minutes, then add the green beans and cook for about 2–3 minutes more until both are tender. Drain and cool under cold running water, then set aside.

3 Mix all the dressing ingredients with some seasoning and pour into the bottom of a large, deep bowl.

4 Layer up the salad on top of the dressing, starting with potatoes, then the beans, salad leaves, shaved cheese and finally the croutons. It is important to layer salad in this order to stop the leaves wilting or the croutons going soggy. Chill, then toss together all the ingredients to serve.

PER SERVING 274 kcals, protein 12g, carbs 28g, fat 13g, sat fat 4g, fibre 2g, sugar 5g, salt 0.62g

Mediterranean fig & mozzarella salad

Smart enough to serve to friends, this inventive salad certainly has the wow factor.
Pour the wonderful dressing over the salad or serve it separately on the side.

TAKES 20 MINUTES • SERVES 4

200g/7oz fine green beans, trimmed
6 small figs, quartered
1 shallot, thinly sliced
1 × 125g ball mozzarella, drained and
    ripped into chunks
50g/2oz hazelnuts, toasted and
    chopped
small handful basil leaves, torn
3 tbsp balsamic vinegar
1 tbsp fig jam or relish
3 tbsp extra virgin olive oil

1 In a large pan of salted water, blanch the beans for 2–3 minutes. Drain, rinse in cold water, then drain on kitchen paper. Arrange on a platter. Top with the figs, shallot, mozzarella, hazelnuts and basil.
2 In a small bowl or a jam jar with a fitted lid, put the vinegar, fig jam or relish, olive oil and some seasoning. Shake well and pour over salad just before serving.

PER SERVING 286 kcals, protein 10g, carbs 11g, fat 23g, sat fat 6g, fibre 3g, sugar 9g, salt 0.3g

Squash, orange & barley salad

This flavourful autumn salad is heart friendly thanks to the cholesterol-balancing fibre in the barley and a phyto-chemical in orange peel, that helps lower blood pressure.

TAKES 1 HOUR 20 MINUTES
● **SERVES 6**

175g/6oz pearl barley
1kg/2lb 4oz peeled squash or
   1 butternut squash, unpeeled
3 tbsp olive oil
zest and juice 1 orange
4 tbsp red wine vinegar
½ red onion, thinly sliced
small bunch mint, chopped, reserving
   a few leaves to garnish
small bunch flat-leaf parsley, chopped,
   reserving a few leaves to garnish
2 handfuls rocket leaves

1 Boil the barley for 20–25 minutes until just tender but with a little bite. Drain and set aside.

2 Meanwhile, heat oven to 200C/180C fan/gas 6. If using butternut, thickly slice into rounds, flicking out the seeds as you go, or slice small, round squashes into thin wedges. Toss with 1 tablespoon of the oil, the orange zest and some seasoning. Spread over a baking sheet and roast for 40 minutes until golden and tender, turning halfway. Set aside while you finish the dish.

3 Mix the orange juice, vinegar and remaining oil with the pearl barley and plenty of seasoning. Stir in the onion and chopped herbs, then layer up on a platter with the squash, rocket and a garnish of the remaining mint and parsley leaves.

PER SERVING 226 kcals, protein 5g, carbs 40g, fat 6g, sat fat 1g, fibre 3g, sugar 9g, salt 0.03g

Lentil & red pepper salad with a soft egg

Just five ingredients and on the table in under 20 minutes – what could be better?
The lentils add a new twist to this light salad.

TAKES 15 MINUTES • SERVES 2

2 eggs
400g can green lentils, rinsed and
    drained
1 small red onion, thinly sliced
1 red pepper, deseeded and finely
    chopped
1 tbsp balsamic vinegar
handful rocket leaves
1 tbsp olive oil

1 Boil the eggs for 6 minutes, then quickly cool under cold running water and peel off the shells. Tip the lentils into a bowl with the onion, red pepper and balsamic vinegar. Mix well.

2 Put the lentil and pepper salad on to a serving dish, then pile the rocket on top. Drizzle with the oil, then halve the eggs and sit them on top of the salad.

PER SERVING 284 kcals, protein 17g, carbs 25g, fat 13g, sat fat 3g, fibre 9g, sugar 8g, salt 1.49g

Chargrilled vegetable salad

Serve these gorgeously flavoured roast vegetables with a cool, creamy soft cheese and some crusty bread for a light lunch or starter.

TAKES 1 HOUR 20 MINUTES

● **SERVES 6**

2 red peppers

3 tbsp olive oil, plus extra for drizzling

1 tbsp red wine vinegar

1 small garlic clove, crushed

1 red chilli, deseeded and finely chopped

1 aubergine, cut into 1cm/½ in rounds

1 large courgette, cut into 1cm/½ in rounds

2 red onions, sliced about 1.5cm/⅔ in thick but kept as whole slices

6 plump sun-dried tomatoes in oil, drained and torn into strips

handful black olives

large handful basil, roughly torn

mozzarella or crumbled feta and crusty bread, to serve (optional)

1 Blacken the peppers all over directly over a flame or under a hot grill. Put them in a bowl, cover and leave to cool.

2 Mix the oil, vinegar, garlic and chilli in a large bowl. On a hot barbecue or griddle pan, chargrill the aubergine, courgette and onions in batches until they have grill marks on both sides and are starting to soften. The time will depend on the intensity of your grill – courgettes and red onions are fine still slightly crunchy but you want the aubergine cooked all the way through. As the vegetables are ready, put them straight into the dressing to marinate, breaking the onions into rings.

3 When the peppers are cool, peel them, remove the stalks and scrape out the seeds. Cut into strips and toss through the veg with any juice from the bowl. Mix in the tomatoes, olives, basil and seasoning. Drizzle with more oil and serve on its own or with mozzarella or crumbled feta and some crusty bread, if you like.

PER SERVING 126 kcals, protein 3g, carbs 10g, fat 9g, sat fat 1g, fibre 4g, sugar 7g, salt 0.66g

Christmas slaw

This salad will keep in the fridge for up to 4 days. Store the dressing separately, then dress the salad just before serving, so the vegetables stay nice and crunchy.

TAKES 15 MINUTES • SERVES 6

FOR THE SALAD

2 carrots, halved
½ white cabbage, shredded
100g/4oz pecan nuts, roughly chopped
bunch spring onions, sliced
2 red peppers, deseeded and sliced

FOR THE DRESSING

2 tbsp maple syrup
2 tsp Dijon mustard
8 tbsp olive oil
4 tbsp cider vinegar

1 Peel strips from the carrots using a vegetable peeler, then mix with the other salad ingredients in a large bowl.

2 Combine all the dressing ingredients in a jam jar, season, then put the lid on and shake well. Toss through the salad when you're ready to eat it.

PER SERVING 312 kcals, protein 4g, carbs 14g, fat 27g, sat fat 3g, fibre 4g, sugar 13g, salt 0.17g

Japanese salad with ginger–soy dressing

This salad counts as two of your 5-a-day. It's a good one to keep in the fridge to graze on with the dressing in a small bowl.

TAKES 30 MINUTES • SERVES 4

4 Baby Gem lettuces, halved
  lengthways
200g/7oz frozen shelled edamame
  (soy) beans, defrosted
4 carrots, cut into long matchsticks
140g/5oz radishes, thinly sliced

FOR THE DRESSING

2 tbsp rice wine vinegar
2 tbsp reduced-salt soy sauce
2 tbsp caster sugar
½ small onion, chopped
2 tsp chopped ginger
1 tbsp tomato purée
2 tbsp vegetable oil

1 Put all the dressing ingredients in a blender or food processor and add 1 tablespoon water. Blend until smooth.
2 Arrange the halved lettuce, edamame, carrots and radishes on four plates or one big platter. When ready to serve, drizzle the dressing over.

PER SERVING 195 kcals, protein 8g, carbs 25g, fat 8g, sat fat 1g, fibre 5g, sugar 19g, salt 1.07g

South-western-style salad

Gone are the days when a salad supper meant a few limp leaves – this exciting, new main-course salad is packed with interesting flavours and textures.

TAKES 30 MINUTES • SERVES 2

2 sweetcorn

400g can black beans, rinsed and drained

1 avocado, cut into chunks

200g/7oz cherry tomatoes, halved

4 spring onions, roughly chopped

100g/4oz feta, crumbled

lime wedges, to garnish (optional)

FOR THE DRESSING

1 tsp ground cumin

1 tbsp chipotle Tabasco (use regular Tabasco if you can't find this)

juice and zest 2 limes

1 tbsp sherry vinegar

2 tbsp extra virgin olive oil

1 Boil the corn for 10 minutes in salted water, rinse in cold water, then cut the kernels off. Tip the beans into a bowl with the cooked corn, avocado, tomatoes and spring onions.

2 Mix the dressing ingredients with some seasoning, then pour over the salad. Toss together well, scatter the feta over the top and serve with lime wedges, if using.

PER SERVING 612 kcals, protein 24g, carbs 47g, fat 38g, sat fat 9g, fibre 9g, sugar 9g, salt 2.83g

Warm squash salad with garlic vinaigrette

You might not have tried squash in a salad before but it works incredibly well with this vinaigrette. Thyme would be a good alternative to the mint.

TAKES 35 MINUTES ● SERVES 4

1 small butternut squash, peeled
3 tbsp olive oil
2 big handfuls rocket leaves
2 × 125g balls mozzarella, torn

FOR THE VINAIGRETTE

2 garlic cloves, thinly sliced
2 tbsp red wine vinegar
1 tbsp honey
small handful mint leaves, chopped

1 Heat oven to 200C/180C fan/gas 6. Slice the squash into 3cm/1 ¼ in pieces. Put on a large, greased baking sheet and drizzle with 1 tablespoon of the oil. Season well and roast for 25 minutes or until golden.

2 While the squash is roasting, make the vinaigrette. Heat the remaining oil in a small pan. Add the garlic, keeping the heat low, and cook until golden. Remove from the heat, and add the vinegar and honey. Return to the heat for 1 minute, whisking until the vinaigrette becomes syrupy, then set aside.

3 To serve, arrange the rocket and mozzarella on four plates. Add the mint to the vinaigrette. Divide the squash among the plates and drizzle with the warm vinaigrette.

PER SERVING 307 kcals, protein 14g, carbs 16g, fat 21g, sat fat 9g, fibre 3g, sugar 9g, salt 0.65g

Cauliflower vinaigrette

Vivid green with a flavour between cauliflower and broccoli, look out for Romanesco cauliflower in shops and markets. If you can't find one, use a small white cauliflower.

TAKES 22 MINUTES • SERVES 8

1 small cauliflower, cut into florets
1 Romanesco cauliflower, cut into
    florets
1 small red onion, very finely chopped
small handful capers, rinsed
handful flat-leaf parsley, chopped

FOR THE DRESSING

6 tbsp olive oil
2 tbsp red wine vinegar
1 tbsp Dijon mustard

1 Make the dressing by whisking all the ingredients together with some seasoning in a large bowl, then set aside.
2 Bring a large pan of water to the boil, cook the cauliflowers for 5–7 minutes until just cooked, then drain well. While the cauliflowers are still hot, toss them with the dressing and leave to cool. Just before serving, add the red onion, capers and parsley.

PER SERVING 114 kcals, protein 3g, carbs 5g, fat 9g, sat fat 1g, fibre 3g, sugar 3g, salt 0.28g

Watermelon & feta salad with crispbread

This combination of sweet watermelon with salty feta is fast becoming a modern classic. Refreshing flavours for a starter or light lunch on warm summer days.

TAKES 1 HOUR, PLUS RISING

● **SERVES 6 AS A STARTER**

½ a watermelon (about 1.5kg/3lb 5oz), peeled, deseeded and cut into chunks

200g block feta, cubed

large handful black olives

handful flat-leaf parsley and mint leaves, roughly chopped

1 red onion, finely sliced into rings

olive oil and balsamic vinegar, to serve

FOR THE CRISPBREAD

½ × 500g pack white bread mix

1 tbsp olive oil, plus a little extra for drizzling

plain flour, for dusting

1 egg white, beaten

a mix of sesame seeds, poppy seeds and fennel seeds, for scattering

1 Make up the bread according to the pack instructions with the olive oil. Leave to rise in a warm place for about 1 hour until doubled in size. Heat oven to 220C/200C fan/gas 7. Knock the bread back and divide into six pieces.

2 On a floured surface, roll the breads out as thinly as possible, then transfer to baking sheets. Brush with the egg white and scatter with the mixed seeds. Bake for about 15 minutes until crisp and brown; if they puff up, even better. You may need to do this in batches. The breads can be made the day before and kept in an airtight container.

3 In a large serving bowl, lightly toss the melon with the feta and olives. Scatter over the herbs and onion rings, then serve with the olive oil and balsamic for drizzling over. Serve the pile of crispbreads on the side for breaking up and scooping up the salad.

PER SERVING 342 kcals, protein 13g, carbs 43g, fat 14g, sat fat 5g, fibre 3g, sugar 13g, salt 1.8g

Nectarine salad with goat's cheese toasts

Fresh, zingy, full of colour and flavour – just what you want to eat on a sunny day. The unusual taste combination really works well.

TAKES 24 MINUTES ● SERVES 4

juice 1 lemon or 2 limes
2 tsp clear honey
1 mild red chilli, deseeded and finely chopped
4 ripe nectarines
8 slices baguette
200g/7oz goat's cheese (choose a log-shaped one)
handful coriander leaves

1 Mix the lemon or lime juice, honey and chilli in a bowl with a little salt. Halve, stone and chop the nectarines, then toss in the dressing.

2 Toast the baguette slices on both sides. Cut the goat's cheese into eight slices and top each toast with a slice.

3 Lift the nectarines into a serving bowl with a slotted spoon and stir through the coriander. Tip the dressing into a small jug and serve alongside the nectarines and goat's cheese toasts.

PER SERVING 291 kcals, protein 13g, carbs 42g, fat 9g, sat fat 5g, fibre 3g, sugar 16g, salt 1.39g

Winter vegetable pie

A great family meal that won't break the budget and is healthy too, as it packs in all five of your 5-a-day. Swap in your own favourite veg.

TAKES 1 HOUR • SERVES 4

2 tbsp olive oil
2 onions, sliced
1 tbsp flour
300g/10oz (about 2 large) carrots, cut into small batons
½ cauliflower, broken into small florets
4 garlic cloves, finely sliced
1 rosemary sprig, leaves finely chopped
400g can chopped tomatoes
200g/7oz frozen peas
900g/2lb potatoes, cut into chunks
up to 200ml/7fl oz milk

1 Heat 1 tablespoon of the oil in a large saucepan over a medium heat. Cook the onions for 10 minutes until softened, then stir in the flour and cook for 2 minutes. Add the carrots, cauliflower, garlic and rosemary, and cook for 5 minutes, stirring, until beginning to soften.

2 Tip the tomatoes into the vegetables with a can full of water. Cover and simmer for 10 minutes, then remove the lid and cook for 10–15 minutes more, until the sauce has thickened and the vegetables are cooked. Season, stir in the peas and cook for 1 minute.

3 Meanwhile, boil the potatoes for 10–15 minutes until tender. Drain, then mash with enough milk to make a fairly soft consistency. Add the remaining oil to the mash and season.

4 Heat the grill. Spoon the hot vegetable mix into a pie dish, top with the mash and drag a fork lightly over the surface. Grill for a few minutes until crisp golden brown.

PER SERVING 388 kcals, protein 15g, carbs 62g, fat 8g, sat fat 2g, fibre 11g, sugar 18g, salt 0.3g

Free-form Florentine pie

A sheet of ready-rolled puff pastry is the basis for this easy-to-make tart. It's a welcome midweek supper for the family when you fancy something different.

TAKES 45 MINUTES • SERVES 4

2 tsp olive oil
400g bag fresh spinach leaves
250g tub ricotta
grating of nutmeg
375g pack ready-rolled puff pastry sheet
4 medium eggs

1 Heat oven to 220C/200C fan/gas 7. Heat the oil in a large pan. Add the spinach and cook until wilted, then drain and thoroughly squeeze out as much liquid as possible. Mix with the ricotta, nutmeg and plenty of seasoning.

2 Lay the pastry on a baking sheet and pinch up the edges to form a lip all round. Prick the base all over with a fork, so the pastry doesn't puff up too much. Bake for 15 minutes or until the pastry is light brown.

3 Remove from the oven and press the pastry down if it has puffed up. Pile in the spinach mix, leaving four clear areas for the eggs to go into. Carefully crack an egg into each space. Season and pop back in the oven for a further 10–15 minutes until the white is set and yolk is still a little runny, or to your taste. Serve the pie immediately.

PER SERVING 587 kcals, protein 20g, carbs 30g, fat 44g, sat fat 18g, fibre 3g, sugar 4g, salt 1.64g

Tagliatelle with vegetable ragu

This low-fat ragu is easily doubled so you can stow some in the freezer for a future meal. Add some chilli pepper and canned beans, and it makes a terrific chilli.

TAKES 50 MINUTES • SERVES 5

1 onion, finely chopped

2 celery sticks, finely chopped

2 carrots, diced

4 garlic cloves, crushed

1 tbsp tomato purée

1 tbsp balsamic vinegar

250g/9oz diced vegetables, such as courgettes, peppers and mushrooms

50g/2oz red split lentils

2 × 400g cans chopped tomatoes with basil

250g/9oz tagliatelle (or your favourite pasta)

2 tbsp shaved vegetarian Parmesan-style cheese (optional)

1 Tip the onion, celery and carrots into a large non-stick pan and add 2–3 tablespoons water, or stock if you have some. Cook gently, stirring often, until the vegetables are soft.

2 Add the garlic, tomato purée and balsamic vinegar, and cook on a high heat for 1 minute more. Add the diced veg, lentils and tomatoes, then bring to the boil. Lower to a simmer, then cook for about 20 minutes.

3 Meanwhile, cook the pasta according to the pack instructions, then drain. Season the ragu and serve with the pasta and some cheese on top, if you like.

PER SERVING 321 kcals, protein 15g, carbs 55g, fat 3g, sat fat 2g, fibre 5g, sugar 12g, salt 0.3g

Fennel & lemon risotto

Creamy and satisfying, risotto is the ultimate comfort food. This new-style recipe is packed with flavour and can easily be doubled.

TAKES 35 MINUTES • SERVES 2

1 large fennel bulb, base trimmed
1 tbsp butter, plus a knob
1 onion, finely chopped
1 garlic clove, finely chopped
140g/5oz risotto rice
175ml/6fl oz white wine
550ml/19fl oz hot vegetable stock
zest 1 lemon
25g/1oz vegetarian Parmesan-style
   cheese, grated

1 Heat oven to 220C/200C fan/gas 7. Chop any green leafy fennel fronds and set aside. Cut off the stalk-like fennel top and reserve, remove the outer layers and finely chop. Heat the 1 tablespoon butter in a frying pan and cook the onion, garlic and chopped fennel until soft but not coloured.

2 Add the rice and stir for 1 minute. Pour over most of the wine and simmer until evaporated. Add 500ml/18 fl oz of the hot stock, a ladleful at a time, stirring between each addition until absorbed.

3 Meanwhile, slice the remaining fennel and fry in the knob of butter until browned. Add the remaining stock and wine, and cook untll tender.

4 When the rice is cooked, stir in the lemon zest, cheese and some seasoning. Take off the heat and set aside, covered, for 2 minutes. Serve in bowls, topped with the fennel fronds and cooked fennel.

PER SERVING 477 kcals, protein 13g, carbs 69g, fat 16g, sat fat 9g, fibre 7g, sugar 12g, salt 1.12g

Sesame & honey tofu with rice noodles

High in protein and low in saturated fat, tofu is an excellent source of immunity-boosting selenium. This Chinese-style stir fry is sure to become a firm favourite.

TAKES 45 MINUTES • SERVES 4

2 tbsp toasted sesame oil

396g pack firm tofu, cut into sticks 1cm × 3cm/½ × 1¼in, and patted dry

150g/5½oz dried brown rice noodles

1 tbsp tamari (gluten-free soy sauce)

2 tsp Chinese five-spice

1 tbsp clear honey

1 red pepper, deseeded and thinly sliced

1 bunch spring onions, cut into fingers

2 heads pak choy (about 200g/7oz), washed and leaves separated

1 Heat half the oil in a frying pan over a medium heat. When hot, add the tofu and cook for 5 minutes on one side. Turn, then fry for another 3 minutes. Continue cooking for 10 minutes more, turning regularly – make sure you scrape up any bits that are stuck. Don't worry if the tofu falls apart a little – these pieces become crispy. Remove to a plate and keep warm.

2 Meanwhile, cook the noodles according to the pack instructions. Drain and set aside. Make dressing by mixing ½ tablespoon oil, the tamari, five-spice and honey.

3 Heat the remaining ½ tablespoon oil in the frying pan and cook the pepper for 1 minute, then add the onions and pak choy. Toss together for 3 minutes, until just wilted. Add the noodles and half the dressing, and mix well. Heat through and divide among four bowls. Top with the tofu and drizzle over the remaining dressing.

PER SERVING 297 kcals, protein 12g, carbs 40g, fat 11g, sat fat 2g, fibre 3g, sugar 9g, salt 1.22g

Butternut macaroni cheese

A favourite with all the family, so why not give macaroni cheese a new twist by adding chunks of roasted squash? Sure to be as popular as the original.

TAKES 50 MINUTES • SERVES 4

1 large butternut squash, peeled and
  cut into 2.5cm/1in chunks
2 tsp olive oil
300g/10oz macaroni
50g/2oz butter
50g/2oz plain flour
1 tsp English mustard powder
500ml/18fl oz milk
200g/7oz extra-mature Cheddar, grated
50g/2oz vegetarian Parmesan-style
  cheese, grated

1 Heat oven to 220C/200C fan/gas 7. Toss the squash with the olive oil and some seasoning, and roast on a baking sheet for 15–20 minutes until tender. Meanwhile, cook the macaroni according to the pack instructions, then drain.

2 Melt the butter in a pan and stir in the flour and mustard powder to make a paste. Gradually whisk in the milk and simmer to thicken and create a smooth sauce, stirring constantly.

3 Take the sauce off the heat and mash in a third of the squash with the Cheddar and half the Parmesan-style cheese. Season, then stir in the drained macaroni with the remaining squash. Tip into an ovenproof dish, scatter with the remaining Parmesan and bake for 15 minutes until golden and bubbling.

PER SERVING 828 kcals, protein 35g, carbs 94g, fat 38g, sat fat 22g, fibre 7g, sugar 19g, salt 1.49g

Mumbai potato wraps with minted-yogurt relish

The chutney, tomatoes and mint sauce give these wraps a sweet, tangy and fresh flavour. Totally delicious and healthy, too!

TAKES 50 MINUTES ● SERVES 4

2 tsp sunflower oil
1 onion, sliced
2 tbsp medium curry powder
400g can chopped tomatoes
750g/1lb 10oz potatoes, diced
2 tbsp spiced mango chutney, plus
 extra to serve (optional)
100g/4oz low-fat natural yogurt
1 tsp mint sauce from a jar
8 plain chapatis
coriander sprigs, to garnish

1 Heat the sunflower oil in a large pan and fry the onion for 6–8 minutes until golden and soft. Stir in 1½ tablespoons of the curry powder, cook for 30 seconds, then add the tomatoes and some seasoning. Simmer, uncovered, for 15 minutes.

2 Meanwhile, add the potatoes and remaining ½ tablespoon of the curry powder to a pan of boiling salted water. Cook for 6–8 minutes until just tender. Drain, reserving 100ml/3½fl oz of the liquid. Add the drained potatoes and reserved liquid to the tomato sauce along with the mango chutney. Heat through.

3 Meanwhile, mix together the yogurt and mint sauce, and warm the chapatis according to the pack instructions.

4 To serve, spoon some of the potatoes on to a chapati and top with a few sprigs of coriander. Drizzle with the minted yogurt relish, adding extra mango chutney, if you wish, then roll up and eat.

PER SERVING 230 kcals, protein 8g, carbs 45g, fat 4g, sat fat 1g, fibre 6g, sugar 10g, salt 0.57g

Ginger sweet tofu with pak choy

Some Chinese dishes can be high in salt due to the soy sauce used. If you want to reduce the salt levels, opt for low-sodium soy sauce.

TAKES 30 MINUTES, PLUS MARINATING • SERVES 2

250g/9oz fresh firm tofu, drained and cut into bite-sized pieces
2 tbsp groundnut oil
1cm/½in piece ginger, sliced
200g/7oz pak choy, leaves separated
1 tbsp Shaohsing rice wine
1 tbsp rice vinegar
½ tsp dried chilli flakes
cooked jasmine rice, to serve

FOR THE MARINADE

1 tbsp grated ginger
1 tsp dark soy sauce
2 tbsp light soy sauce
1 tbsp brown sugar

1 Gently prick a few holes in the tofu with a toothpick. Mix the marinade ingredients together and toss in the tofu. Marinate for 10–15 minutes.

2 Heat a wok over a high heat and add half the oil. When the oil starts to smoke, stir-fry the ginger for a few seconds. Add the pak choy and stir-fry for 1–2 minutes. Add a splash of water and cook for 2 minutes. When the leaves have wilted and the stems are cooked, season with salt and transfer to a serving dish.

3 Add the remaining oil to the wok and when it starts to smoke, add the tofu (retaining the marinade liquid) and stir-fry for 5–10 minutes. Take care not to break up the tofu as you toss it to get it evenly browned. Season with rice wine and vinegar. Add the remaining marinade, bring to a bubble and let the liquid reduce.

4 Sprinkle over the chilli flakes and toss well. Spoon the tofu on to the pak choy and serve immediately with rice.

PER SERVING 241 kcals, protein 11g, carbs 16g, fat 15g, sat fat 3g, fibre 1g, sugar 11g, salt 3.47g

Grilled aubergines with spicy chickpeas

This easily doubled dish has great textures and tastes – creamy, smoky aubergine, nutty chickpeas and earthy walnuts.

TAKES 50 MINUTES ● SERVES 2

4 tbsp olive oil

1 onion, finely chopped

1 red chilli, deseeded and finely chopped

2cm/¾in piece ginger, finely chopped

½ tsp each ground cumin, coriander and cinnamon

400g can chickpeas, rinsed and drained

200g/7oz tomatoes, chopped

juice ½ lemon

2 aubergines, sliced lengthways

FOR THE WALNUT SAUCE

200g tub Greek-style yogurt

1 garlic clove, crushed

25g/1oz walnuts, chopped

handful coriander leaves, roughly chopped

1 Heat 2 tablespoons oil in a pan, add the onion and fry until soft and lightly browned, about 10 minutes. Add the chilli, ginger and spices, and mix well. Stir in the chickpeas, tomatoes and 5 tablespoons water, bring to the boil, then simmer for 10 minutes. Add a little salt and pepper and the lemon juice.

2 Heat the grill. Arrange the aubergines over a grill pan. Brush lightly with some of the remaining oil, sprinkle with salt and pepper, then grill until golden. Flip them over, brush the other side with oil, season and grill again until tender and golden.

3 Mix the yogurt with the garlic, most of the walnuts and coriander and a little salt and pepper. Arrange the aubergine slices over a warm platter and spoon over the chickpea mix. Drizzle with the walnut sauce and scatter with the remaining walnuts and coriander.

PER SERVING 640 kcals, protein 22g, carbs 39g, fat 45g, sat fat 10g, fibre 13g, sugar 16g, salt 0.9g

Cheesy bean burgers

Coating the burgers in breadcrumbs gives them a lovely golden crunchy coating, but if you're pushed for time, just dust with a little flour.

TAKES 40 MINUTES, PLUS CHILLING
● **SERVES 2**

400g can butter beans, rinsed and
    drained
3 tbsp olive oil
1 small onion, finely chopped
1 garlic clove, crushed
75g/2½oz Wensleydale cheese,
    crumbled
300g punnet cherry tomatoes
1 tbsp plain flour
1 egg, beaten
50g/2oz fresh white breadcrumbs
100g bag rocket leaves

1 Heat oven to 190C/170C fan/gas 5. Tip the butter beans into a bowl and mash with a fork to form a rough purée. Set aside. Heat 1 tablespoon of the oil in a small pan and cook the onion and garlic gently for 3–4 minutes, until softened.

2 Stir the onion mixture into the butter beans, along with the cheese, then season. Shape the mixture into four patties, cover and chill for 10 minutes.

3 Put the tomatoes in a small roasting tin and season with salt and pepper. Roast for 10–15 minutes, until tender.

4 Tip the flour, egg and breadcrumbs on to three separate plates. Roll each patty in the flour, dusting off any excess, then roll in the egg, and finally coat in breadcrumbs.

5 Heat the remaining oil in a non-stick frying pan and add the burgers. Cook for 8–10 minutes, turning occasionally until golden. Drain on kitchen paper and serve with the roasted tomatoes and rocket.

PER SERVING 541 kcals, protein 23g, carbs 41g, fat 33g, sat fat 11g, fibre 7g, sugar 4g, salt 2.36g

Veggie Bolognese

Always a favourite with family or friends, this spag Bol uses Quorn – a tasty low-fat, high-protein meat alternative.

TAKES 40 MINUTES • SERVES 4

2 tbsp olive oil
1 onion, chopped
1 large carrot, diced
200g/7oz mushrooms, thickly sliced
400g can chopped tomatoes
1 tsp dried mixed herbs
2 tbsp tomato ketchup
1 tbsp vegetable stock concentrate
350g pack Quorn mince
400g/14oz spaghetti
grated vegetarian Parmesan-style
   cheese, to garnish

1 Heat the oil in a large frying pan, add the onion and carrot, and cook, stirring frequently, for about 10 minutes until the onion is soft. Add the mushrooms and stir-fry for a few minutes more.

2 Tip the tomatoes into the pan with half a can of water, the herbs, ketchup and stock, then stir well to make a sauce.

3 Stir the Quorn into the sauce, season with salt and pepper, then cover and simmer for 12 minutes until the vegetables are cooked and the mixture is saucy rather than wet.

4 Meanwhile, bring a large pan of salted water to the boil. Add the spaghetti and cook according to the pack instructions – usually about 9–10 minutes – until just tender. Drain the spaghetti and pile into four warmed bowls. Spoon the sauce on top, then generously grate over the cheese before serving.

PER SERVING 582 kcals, protein 33g, carbs 87g, fat 14g, sat fat 4g, fibre 10g, sugar 11g, salt 1.92g

Cauliflower & chickpea pilaf

A hearty, tasty and very simple meal – increase the amount of curry paste if you like things spicy. This dish counts as three of your 5-a-day.

TAKES 30 MINUTES • SERVES 4

1 tbsp sunflower oil
2 large onions, sliced
1 tbsp curry paste of your choice
200g/7oz basmati rice
350g/12oz cauliflower florets
400g can chickpeas, rinsed and drained
500ml/18fl oz vegetable stock
50g/2oz toasted flaked almonds
handful chopped coriander leaves

1 Heat the oil in a large non-stick pan and add the onions. Cook over a medium heat for 5 minutes until starting to turn golden. Stir in the curry paste and cook for 1 minute. Add the rice, cauliflower and chickpeas, stirring to coat in the paste.

2 Pour in the stock and stir. Cover and simmer for 10–15 minutes until the rice and cauliflower are tender and all the liquid has been absorbed. Stir in the almonds and coriander, then serve.

PER SERVING 443 kcals, protein 16g, carbs 68g, fat 14g, sat fat 1g, fibre 8g, sugar 10g, salt 0.82g

Veggie shepherd's pie with sweet potato mash

Choose big, old carrots (old as in mature, rather than past their best!) so they don't lose their texture when cooked. Sweet potato is a colourful alternative to normal mash.

TAKES 45 MINUTES • SERVES 4

1 tbsp olive oil
1 large onion, sliced
2 really large carrots (500g/1lb 2oz in total), cut into sugar-cube sized pieces
2 tbsp chopped thyme leaves
200ml/7fl oz red wine
400g can chopped tomatoes
2 vegetable stock cubes
410g can green lentils
950g/2lb 2oz sweet potatoes, peeled and cut into chunks
25g/1oz butter
85g/3oz mature Cheddar, grated
steamed broccoli, to serve

1 Heat the oil in a frying pan, then fry the onion until golden. Add the carrots and all but a sprinkling of thyme. Pour in the wine, 150ml/¼ pint water and the tomatoes, then sprinkle in the stock cubes and simmer for 10 minutes. Tip in the can of lentils, including their juice, then cover and simmer for another 10 minutes until the carrots still have a bit of bite and the lentils are pulpy.

2 Heat oven to 190C/170C fan/gas 5. Meanwhile, boil the sweet potatoes for 15 minutes until tender, drain well, then mash with the butter and season to taste. Pile the lentil mixture into a pie dish, spoon the mash on top, then sprinkle over the grated cheese and remaining thyme.

3 Cook for 20 minutes until golden and hot all the way through. Serve with steamed broccoli.

PER SERVING 531 kcals, protein 16g, carbs 79g, fat 17g, sat fat 8g, fibre 12g, sugar 31g, salt 3.95g

Yellow lentil & coconut curry with cauliflower

This curry is low calorie, a good source of fibre and iron, and counts as two of your 5-a-day.

TAKES 1 HOUR 5 MINUTES ● SERVES 4

1 tbsp vegetable oil
1 onion, thinly sliced
2 garlic cloves, crushed
thumb-sized piece ginger, finely
   chopped
3 tbsp curry paste
200g/7oz yellow lentils, rinsed
1.5 litres/2¾ pints vegetable stock
3 tbsp unsweetened desiccated
   coconut, plus extra to sprinkle
1 cauliflower, broken into little florets
cooked basmati rice and coriander
   leaves, plus mango chutney and
   naan bread, to serve

1 Heat the oil in a large pan, then add the onion, garlic and ginger. Cook for 5 minutes, add the curry paste, then stir-fry for 1 minute before adding the lentils, stock and coconut. Bring the mixture to the boil and simmer for 40 minutes or until the lentils are soft.

2 During the final 10 minutes of cooking, stir in the cauliflower to cook.

3 Spoon the rice into four bowls, top with the curry and sprinkle with coriander leaves and the extra coconut. Serve with mango chutney and naan bread.

PER SERVING 356 kcals, protein 18g, carbs 33g, fat 17g, sat fat 9g, fibre 10g, sugar 9g, salt 1.4g

Cheat's deep-pan pizza

Vary the topping on this pizza with your own favourites. It can be frozen after cooking for up to a month. Thaw, wrap in foil and reheat in a low oven.

TAKES 50 MINUTES • SERVES 6

500g/1lb 2oz self-raising flour
1 tbsp baking powder
100g/4oz butter, diced
300ml/½ pint milk
2 tbsp olive oil, plus extra for brushing
handful semi-dried tomatoes
2 small courgettes, thickly sliced
½ × 300g jar chargrilled artichokes in oil, drained
125g ball mozzarella, drained and diced
50g/2oz mature Cheddar, grated
½ tsp dried oregano or rosemary

1 Heat oven to 200C/180C fan/gas 6. Mix the flour, baking powder and ½ teaspoon salt in a large bowl, then rub in the butter. Add the milk and bring together to make a soft, slightly sticky dough. Brush a 25 × 36cm (10 × 14in) baking sheet with a little olive oil and press the dough into it, making sure it goes right to the corners.

2 Arrange the tomatoes, courgettes and artichokes over the base. Scatter over the cheeses, drizzle with the oil and sprinkle with the oregano or rosemary. Season with pepper. Bake for 25 minutes until nicely browned and serve immediately.

PER SERVING 589 kcals, protein 16g, carbs 69g, fat 30g, sat fat 15g, fibre 3g, sugar 5g, salt 2.85g

Herby chickpea balls with tomato sauce

The chickpea balls have a fantastic taste with a good kick of garlic. Oil your hands with a little cooking oil when shaping the balls to stop the mixture sticking.

TAKES 35 MINUTES • SERVES 3

2 slices white bread, crusts off and torn into pieces
75g/2½oz vegetarian Parmesan-style cheese, 50g roughly chopped and 25g grated
400g can chickpeas, rinsed and drained
3 garlic cloves, 2 roughly chopped and 1 crushed
2 tsp dried oregano
small handful basil leaves, chopped
1 egg, beaten
1 tbsp olive oil, plus extra for greasing
560ml jar passata with onions and garlic
200g/7oz fusilli spaghetti, linguine or tagliatelle

1 Heat oven to 220C/200C fan/gas 7. Whizz the bread and roughly chopped cheese to crumbs in a food processor, then throw in the chickpeas, roughly chopped garlic, half the oregano, a few basil leaves and some seasoning. Pulse until the mixture starts to come together, then add just enough of the egg while the motor is running to bind together. Shape into 18 small balls. Transfer to an oiled baking sheet and cook in the oven for 15 minutes, turning halfway.

2 Meanwhile, in a large pan, fry the crushed garlic in the olive oil for 1 minute. Then tip in the passata, remaining oregano and some seasoning, and simmer until the chickpea balls are ready. Cook the pasta according to the pack instructions.

3 When the chickpea balls are cooked, serve over the pasta, with the tomato sauce and the rest of the basil on top. Sprinkle with the grated cheese.

PER SERVING 607 kcals, protein 30g, carbs 85g, fat 19g, sat fat 6g, fibre 6g, sugar 9g, salt 2.15g

Chickpea, tomato & spinach curry

This well-balanced, superhealthy curry is suitable for vegans and contains two of your 5-a-day. You can use any kind of canned beans instead of the chickpeas, if you prefer.

TAKES 55 MINUTES • SERVES 6

1 onion, chopped
2 garlic cloves, chopped
3cm/1¼in piece ginger, grated
6 ripe tomatoes, chopped
½ tbsp oil
1 tsp ground cumin
2 tsp ground coriander
1 tsp ground turmeric
pinch chilli flakes
1 tsp yeast extract (we used Marmite)
4 tbsp red split lentils
6 tbsp coconut cream
1 head broccoli, broken into small
   florets
400g can chickpeas, rinsed and drained
100g bag baby leaf spinach
1 lemon, halved
1 tbsp toasted sesame seeds mixed
   with 1 tbsp chopped cashew nuts
boiled brown rice, to serve (optional)

1 Put the onion, garlic, ginger and tomatoes in a food processor or blender and whizz to a purée.

2 Heat the oil in a large pan. Add the spices, fry for a few seconds and add the purée mixture and yeast extract. Bubble together for 2 minutes, then add the lentils and coconut cream. Cook until the lentils are tender, then add the broccoli and cook for 4 minutes. Stir in the chickpeas and spinach, squeeze over the lemon halves and swirl through the sesame and cashew mixture. Serve with brown rice, if you like.

PER SERVING 199 kcals, protein 8g, carbs 18g, fat 10g, sat fat 5g, fibre 5g, sugar 6g, salt 0.42g

Risotto with peas & broad beans

The first broad beans in spring are so tender and sweet that it's best to use them as simply as possible – in a risotto or a seasonal salad.

TAKES 35 MINUTES • SERVES 4

1 tbsp olive oil
100g/4oz cold butter, diced
1 small onion or 2 shallots, chopped
175g/6oz risotto rice
100ml/3½fl oz white wine
600ml/1 pint hot vegetable stock
200g/7oz fresh peas, podded (about
  1kg/2lb 4oz unpodded weight)
200g/7oz broad beans, podded (about
  1kg/2lb 4oz unpodded weight)
50g/2oz vegetarian Parmesan-style
  cheese, finely grated

1 Heat the oil and 25g/1oz of the butter in a large pan over a medium heat. Add the onion or shallots and cook until soft and translucent, about 4–5 minutes. Stir in the rice and cook for a further 2 minutes. Turn up the heat and add the wine, let it bubble to evaporate the alcohol.

2 Once the wine has reduced, begin adding the hot stock a ladle at a time over a medium heat, allowing each addition to be absorbed before adding the next and stirring continuously. The rice should always be moist, but not swimming in liquid. This process should take 16–20 minutes, depending on what kind of risotto rice you use.

3 Bring a pan of salted water to the boil and blanch the peas and beans for 2–3 minutes. Drain and set aside. Remove the risotto from the heat and stir in the remaining butter, cheese, peas and beans with some seasoning before serving.

PER SERVING 476 kcals, protein 12g, carbs 44g, fat 28g, sat fat 16g, fibre 4g, sugar 4g, salt 0.92g

Chard, sweet potato & peanut stew

The ground peanuts add a surprising richness and up the protein content of this dish. Serve the stew on its own in bowls, or with rice.

TAKES 1 HOUR • SERVES 4

2 tbsp sunflower oil

1 large onion, chopped

1 tsp cumin seeds

400g/14oz sweet potatoes, cut into medium chunks

½ tsp crushed chilli flakes

400g can chopped tomatoes

140g/5oz salted roasted peanuts

250g/9oz chard, leaves and stems, washed and roughly chopped

1 Heat a large saucepan with a lid over a medium heat and add the oil. Add the onion and fry until light golden. Stir in the cumin seeds until fragrant, about 1 minute, then add the sweet potatoes, chilli flakes, tomatoes and 750ml/1¼ pints water. Stir, cover and bring to the boil, then uncover and simmer for 15 minutes.

2 Meanwhile, whizz the peanuts in a food processor until finely ground, but stop before you end up with peanut butter. Add them to the stew, stir and taste for seasoning – you may want to add a pinch more salt. Simmer for a further 15 minutes, stirring frequently.

3 Finally, stir in the chard. Return to the boil and simmer, covered, stirring occasionally, for 8–10 minutes or until the chard is cooked. Serve the stew piping hot with plenty of freshly ground black pepper.

PER SERVING 398 kcals, protein 13g, carbs 33g, fat 25g, sat fat 4g, fibre 6g, sugar 12g, salt 0.93g

Spiced rice & beans

This is a version of an Indian dish called kitchari and is a great storecupboard supper. The tomato topping adds a refreshing tang to the spicy rice.

TAKES 40 MINUTES • SERVES 4

200g/7oz basmati rice

2 tbsp oil

1 onion, chopped

2cm/¾in piece ginger, chopped

2 garlic cloves, finely chopped

1 green chilli, deseeded and finely chopped

1 tsp each cumin and mustard seeds

400g can black eye beans/peas, rinsed and drained

2 bay leaves

1 cinnamon stick

1 tsp ground turmeric

2 tbsp pumpkin seeds, plain or toasted, to garnish

TOMATO TOPPING

300g/10oz tomatoes, chopped

1 tsp grated ginger

½ red onion, finely chopped

1 Rinse the rice several times in cold water until the water runs clear. Drain well. Heat the oil in a large pan, add the onion and ginger, and fry for 5 minutes until the onion is lightly coloured. Stir in the garlic, chilli, cumin and mustard seeds, and fry for 1 minute.

2 Tip the rice and beans/peas into the pan and mix well. Add 600ml/1 pint water, the bay leaves, cinnamon stick, turmeric and a little salt. Bring to the boil, then reduce the heat, cover and cook gently for about 15 minutes until the rice is tender.

3 Meanwhile, mix together the tomatoes, ginger and red onion for the topping with plenty of freshly ground black pepper and a little salt. Serve the rice and beans/peas in warmed bowls topped with the tomato mixture and sprinkled with pumpkin seeds.

PER SERVING 332 kcals, protein 11g, carbs 56g, fat 9g, sat fat 1g, fibre 3g, sugar 3g, salt 0.58g

Cheese soufflé & winter salad

Soufflés aren't difficult to make, so give this one a go. It's basically a cheese sauce with whisked egg whites mixed in. The salad makes a perfect partner.

TAKES 1 HOUR • SERVES 4

FOR THE SOUFFLÉ

50g/2oz butter, plus extra for greasing

25g/1oz plain flour, plus extra for dusting

200ml/7fl oz milk

300g/10oz leftover hard cheese, cut into chunks

100ml/3½fl oz double cream or crème fraîche

4 eggs, separated

grating of nutmeg

pinch cayenne pepper

FOR THE SALAD

110g bag salad leaves

100g/4oz blue or goat's cheese, crumbled

50g/2oz walnuts

1 pear, sliced

3 tbsp salad dressing (use your favourite)

1 Heat oven to 200C/180C fan/gas 6. Melt all the butter in a pan. Brush a 20cm soufflé dish with a little of it, then dust the dish with the extra flour. Stir the 25g/1oz flour into the rest of the melted butter in the saucepan, then sizzle for 1 minute. Gradually pour in the milk to make a white sauce, then add two-thirds of the cheese and carry on cooking to melt. Leave to cool slightly, then mix in the remaining cheese, the cream or crème fraîche and the egg yolks. Season, then add the nutmeg and cayenne pepper.

2 In a clean bowl, whisk the egg whites until stiff. Fold into the cheese sauce, then carefully tip into the soufflé dish. Bake the soufflé for 25 minutes until puffed up and golden.

3 While the soufflé is cooking, toss the salad ingredients together. Once the soufflé is cooked, dress the salad and serve alongside.

PER SERVING 840 kcals, protein 37g, carbs 13g, fat 71g, sat fat 40g, fibre 2g, sugar 8g, salt 2.3g

Baked goat's cheese with hazelnut crust

This makes a very easy starter. As a change from the onions, you could serve the nutty cheeses with a crisp apple salad tossed in a hazelnut oil and lemon dressing.

TAKES 55 MINUTES • SERVES 6

3 × 100g goat's cheese
50g/2oz hazelnuts, chopped
25g/1oz breadcrumbs
2 eggs, beaten
red chicory leaves, watercress and
   rocket leaves, to serve

FOR THE ONIONS

3 tbsp olive oil
3 red onions, halved and thinly sliced
4 tbsp balsamic vinegar
4 tbsp mild-flavoured clear honey

1 Halve the goat's cheeses horizontally and mix the nuts with the crumbs. Coat the cheese in the egg, then the nut mixture. Mark the cut-side of the cheese with a large piece of nut to show which side up it should be.

2 For the onions, heat the oil in a non-stick pan, then add the onions. Stir well and cook for 10 minutes until softened and starting to turn golden. Tip in the vinegar and honey, season and stir over the heat until syrupy.

3 Heat oven to 200C/180C fan/gas 6. Put the cheese on a sheet of baking parchment on a baking sheet and bake for 20 minutes. Arrange the salad leaves on plates and spoon the onions on top. Add the goat's cheese, drizzle with any juice from the onions and serve immediately.

PER SERVING 366 kcals, protein 14g, carbs 17g, fat 28g, sat fat 11g, fibre 1g, sugar 12g, salt 1.05g

Spicy paneer skewers

Gram flour, made from ground chickpeas, has a lovely nutty flavour and is used extensively in Indian cookery. If you can't get hold of paneer, tofu is also good.

TAKES 25 MINUTES, PLUS MARINATING • SERVES 10

600g/1lb 5oz paneer cheese
juice 2 lemons
2 tsp ground cumin, plus extra for
  sprinkling
75g/2½oz gram flour
1 tsp garam masala
1 tbsp paprika
284ml tub double cream
4 garlic cloves, crushed
2 red chillies, deseeded and chopped
2 peppers (1 red and 1 yellow),
  deseeded and roughly chopped
2 courgettes, sliced
25g/1oz butter, melted
2 lemons, cut into wedges

1 Soak 12–15 bamboo skewers in water for 15 minutes – this helps to stop them burning under the grill. Cut the paneer into 3cm/1¼in cubes and toss with lemon juice and cumin. Set aside for 30 minutes.
2 Sift the gram flour, garam masala and paprika into a bowl and add the cream, garlic and chillies, plus enough water to make a thick batter, then stir until smooth. Drain the paneer, reserving the cumin-spiced juices, and add to the batter with 2 tablespoons of the juice. Coat all the paneer cubes in batter.
3 Heat the grill to high and line the grill pan with foil. Thread the paneer on to skewers, alternating it with chunks of pepper and courgette. Drizzle with batter from the bowl and cook for 4–5 minutes on each side, spooning over more batter when you turn them. Grill until charred at the edges. Brush with melted butter, sprinkle with cumin, and serve immediately with lemon wedges.

PER SERVING 421 kcals, protein 17g, carbs 10g, fat 35g, sat fat 22g, fibre 2g, sugar 4g, salt 0.1g

Veggie rice pot

Forget the takeaway and make your own Chinese special rice at home. You can add all sorts of other veg to this too, such as beansprouts, broccoli florets and baby corn.

TAKES 35 MINUTES • SERVES 4

1 tbsp sunflower or groundnut oil
2 peppers (1 red, 1 yellow), deseeded
   and thickly sliced
250g pack shiitake or chestnut
   mushrooms, sliced
250g/9oz long grain rice (not the
   easy-cook type)
2 garlic cloves, finely chopped
1 heaped tsp five-spice powder
3 tbsp dry sherry
140g/5oz frozen petits pois
1 tsp sesame oil
2 eggs, beaten
bunch spring onions, sliced diagonally
1 tbsp light soy sauce, or more if
   you like

1 Boil the kettle. Heat the oil in a large, deep frying pan, then add the peppers and mushrooms. Fry over a high heat for 3 minutes or until starting to soften and turn golden. Turn down the heat, then stir in the rice, garlic and five-spice. Sizzle for 2 minutes, then splash in the sherry and top up with 350ml/12fl oz hot water.

2 Cover the pan and simmer for 15–20 minutes until all of the liquid has been absorbed and the rice is tender, stirring now and again. Add the peas for the final few minutes.

3 Heat another frying pan, add a drop of the sesame oil, then add the eggs. Swirl them around the pan to make a thin omelette. Once set, turn out on to a board, roll up and shred thinly. Tip the egg and spring onions on to the rice, fluff up with a fork, season with soy sauce and the remaining sesame oil, then serve.

PER SERVING 377 kcals, protein 12g, carbs 67g, fat 9g, sat fat 2g, fibre 4g, sugar 9g, salt 1.14g

Festive squash jalousie

This makes a good centrepiece for a special meal and the flavours work well with traditional Christmas vegetables such as roasties, Brussels and steamed carrots.

TAKES 2 HOURS ● SERVES 6

1 large butternut squash, peeled, deseeded and chopped into chunks
4 garlic cloves, skin on, bashed
rosemary sprig, leaves stripped and chopped
few thyme sprigs, leaves stripped
3 tbsp olive oil
1 onion, chopped
1 large field mushroom, chopped
125g pack cooked chestnuts, broken into large pieces
2 tbsp chopped parsley
1 tbsp chopped sage
250g tub mascarpone cheese
1 tbsp grated vegetarian Parmesan-style cheese
pinch freshly grated nutmeg
500g pack puff pastry
1 egg, beaten

1 Heat oven to 200C/180C fan/gas 6. Toss the squash in a roasting tin with the garlic, rosemary and thyme. Drizzle with oil. Season. Roast for 40 minutes. Remove and squeeze the garlic out of its skin, mash and mix with the squash.

2 Fry the onion until soft. Add the mushroom and fry for 3–4 minutes. Remove and set aside. Mix together the chestnuts, herbs, cheeses and nutmeg. Stir in the mushroom and squash. Season.

3 Roll a third of the pastry into a 12 × 30cm/4½ × 12in rectangle. Place on a baking sheet. Pierce all over with a fork, brush with egg and bake for 10 minutes.

4 Roll out the remaining pastry to a slightly larger rectangle and slash diagonally. Pile the filling on to the partly cooked base, leaving a 1cm/½in border. Brush the border with egg and lay the uncooked pastry on top, pressing down the edges to seal. Glaze with the remaining egg. Bake for 30–35 minutes until cooked.

PER SERVING 694 kcals, protein 10g, carbs 50g, fat 52g, sat fat 25g, fibre 5g, sugar 12g, salt 1.04g

Wild mushroom & chestnut cottage pie

This hearty dish is a wonderful veggie cottage pie using flavourful wild mushrooms. Serve it with some buttered kale or greens for a casual supper with friends.

TAKES 1 HOUR 20 MINUTES

● **SERVES 4**

2 tbsp vegetable oil
2 carrots, chopped
½ swede, peeled and chopped
12 pearl onions, peeled and left whole
1 garlic clove, crushed
1 rosemary sprig
1 tsp tomato purée
1 tsp yeast extract, such as Marmite
200g can chopped tomatoes
50ml/2fl oz white wine
175ml/6fl oz vegetable stock
500g/1lb 2oz mixed wild mushrooms, roughly chopped
200g/7oz vacuum-packed chestnuts, halved

FOR THE TOPPING

3 potatoes, peeled and diced
2 parsnips, peeled and diced
2 carrots, diced
300g/10oz celeriac, peeled and diced
100g/4oz butter
50ml/2fl oz milk

1 Heat the oil in a large frying pan, add the carrots, swede and onions, and cook for 8 minutes. Add the garlic, rosemary, tomato purée and yeast extract, and cook for a further 5 minutes. Add the tomatoes and wine, and scrape all the goodness off the bottom of the pan. Pour in the stock, add the mushrooms and chestnuts, then simmer for 8 minutes until the sauce is reduced and thickened. Remove from the heat and cool slightly.

2 Meanwhile, to make the topping, put all the vegetables in a large pan of salted water and bring to the boil. Cook for 12 minutes or until the vegetables are tender. Drain, then allow to steam-dry for 5 minutes. Roughly mash the roots with butter, milk and some seasoning.

3 Heat oven to 190C/170C fan/gas 5. Pile the mushroom mixture into an ovenproof dish, top with the mash, then cook for 30 minutes until golden and bubbling.

PER SERVING 538 kcals, protein 11g, carbs 59g, fat 30g, sat fat 14g, fibre 15g, sugar 25g, salt 1.05g

Tofu & spinach cannelloni

Protein-rich tofu is made from soya milk and can be used in all kinds of dishes.
It's low in fat and helps to lower cholesterol too.

TAKES 1 HOUR 25 MINUTES

● **SERVES 6**

2 tbsp olive oil

1 onion, chopped

3 garlic cloves, finely chopped

2 × 400g cans chopped tomatoes

50g/2oz pine nuts, roughly chopped

400g bag spinach leaves

350g pack silken tofu

pinch grated nutmeg

300g pack fresh lasagne sheets

4 tbsp fresh breadcrumbs

1 Heat half the oil in a pan, add the onion and one-third of the garlic, fry until softened. Pour in the tomatoes, season and bring to the boil. Reduce the heat and cook for 10 minutes.

2 Heat half the remaining oil in a frying pan and cook another third of the garlic for 1 minute, then add half the pine nuts and all the spinach. Wilt the spinach, then tip out the excess liquid. Whizz the tofu in a food processor until smooth, then stir through the spinach with the nutmeg and some pepper. Remove from the heat and allow to cool slightly.

3 Heat oven to 200C/180C fan/gas 6. Pour half the tomato sauce into a 20 × 30cm ovenproof dish. Divide the spinach mix among the lasagne sheets, roll up and lay them on top of the sauce. Pour over the remaining sauce. Bake for 30 minutes.

4 Mix the crumbs with the remaining garlic and pine nuts. Sprinkle over the dish, drizzle with oil and bake for 10 minutes.

PER SERVING 284 kcals, protein 13g, carbs 30g, fat 13g, sat fat 2g, fibre 4g, sugar 6g, salt 0.65g

Shallot tarte Tatin with goat's cheese

The sweet flavour of the caramelised shallots and their sticky juices is offset by slices of tangy goat's cheese. Serve this Tatin simply with some green salad leaves.

TAKES 1 HOUR 25 MINUTES
● **SERVES 4–5**

600g/1lb 5oz shallots
2 tbsp olive oil
25g/1oz butter
4 tbsp balsamic vinegar
2 tbsp demerara or light soft brown sugar
4 thyme sprigs
375g ready-rolled puff pastry
100–140g/4–5oz goat's cheese, sliced into rounds (we used 140g/5oz)

1 Heat oven to 200C/180C fan/gas 6. Put the shallots into a heatproof bowl and pour over boiling water to cover. Leave for 10 minutes, then drain and peel.

2 Heat the oil and butter in a frying pan. Add the shallots and fry gently for 10–15 minutes. Stir in the vinegar and sugar with the leaves from two thyme sprigs for a few minutes until caramelised. Turn off the heat and season.

3 Tear the remaining thyme sprigs into a few pieces and scatter over the base of a 22cm ovenproof shallow pan, cake or tart tin – without a loose base. Tip in the shallots with all their sticky juices.

4 Roll out the pastry until it is big enough to cut out a roughly 26cm/10in circle. Lift the pastry circle onto the shallots, then tuck the edges down the inside of the tin.

5 Bake for 25–30 minutes. Leave the tart for 5 minutes to settle, then turn out of the tin. Dot with rounds of goat's cheese and slice into wedges.

PER SERVING (4) 603 kcals, protein 14g, carbs 39g, fat 45g, sat fat 20g, fibre 3g, sugar 16g, salt 1.56g

Pumpkin, cranberry & red onion tagine

This dish is warming, hearty and delicious, with the sweet-and-sour flavours working beautifully. The accompanying couscous has a lovely citrus zing.

TAKES 45 MINUTES • SERVES 4

3 tbsp olive oil

2 red onions, thickly sliced

3cm/1¼in piece ginger, grated

500g/1lb 2oz pumpkin or squash, peeled, deseeded and cut into large chunks

1 tsp each ground cinnamon, coriander and cumin

1 tsp harissa paste

1 tbsp clear honey

700g bottle tomato passata

50g/2oz dried cranberries

400g can chickpeas, rinsed and drained

200g/7oz couscous

2 tsp vegetable stock granules

zest and juice 1 lemon

3 tbsp toasted flaked almonds

handful coriander, roughly chopped, to garnish

1 Heat 2 tablespoons of the oil in a pan and fry the onions until lightly coloured. Add the ginger, pumpkin or squash, spices and harissa, stir, then add the honey, passata and cranberries. Bring to the boil.

2 Reduce the heat, cover, then simmer for 20 minutes until the pumpkin is tender. After 10 minutes, stir in the chickpeas. (If the mixture is a little thick, loosen it with some vegetable stock.)

3 Meanwhile, tip the couscous, stock granules and lemon zest into a heatproof bowl. Pour over 300ml/½ pint boiling water, stir briefly and cover with a plate. Leave for 5 minutes. Tip in the lemon juice, almonds and remaining tablespoon of oil and fluff up with a fork. Serve the couscous with the tagine and scatter over the coriander.

PER SERVING 449 kcals, protein 13g, carbs 67g, fat 16g, sat fat 2g, fibre 6g, sugar 23g, salt 1.93g

Black bean chilli

Comforting, delicious and healthy. The cumin and cider vinegar add a lovely dimension to this great stew-like winter dish.

TAKES 40 MINUTES • SERVES 4–6

2 tbsp olive oil
4 garlic cloves, finely chopped
2 large onions, chopped
3 tbsp sweet pimentón (Spanish paprika) or mild chilli powder
3 tbsp ground cumin
3 tbsp cider vinegar
2 tbsp brown sugar
2 × 400g cans chopped tomatoes
2 × 400g cans black beans, rinsed and drained
boiled long grain rice
plus a few, or one, of the following toppings to serve: crumbled feta, chopped spring onions, sliced radishes, avocado chunks, soured cream

1 In a large pan, heat the olive oil and fry the garlic and onions for 5 minutes until almost softened. Add the pimentón and cumin, cook for a few minutes, then add the vinegar, sugar, tomatoes and some seasoning. Cook for 10 minutes.

2 Pour in the beans and cook for another 10 minutes. Serve with rice and the accompaniments of your choice in small bowls. Let guests add their own topping to their chilli.

PER SERVING (4) 339 kcals, protein 17g, carbs 50g, fat 10g, sat fat 1g, fibre 8g, sugar 20g, salt 1.45g

Vegetable subzi biryani

Aromatic rather than spicy, this classic biryani just needs chutneys, poppadums and Indian beer for a deliciously authentic curry night.

TAKES 2 HOURS, PLUS SOAKING
• **SERVES 6**

400g/14oz basmati rice, washed, then
   left to soak in water for 1 hour
125ml/4fl oz sunflower oil
4 large onions, sliced
small knob ginger, finely grated to
   make 1 tsp
1 garlic clove, crushed
225g/8oz tomatoes, skinned and
   finely chopped
1 tsp red chilli powder
1 tsp ground turmeric
1 cinnamon stick
4 cardamom pods
1 tsp cumin seeds
1 tsp black peppercorns
1 tsp cloves
4 star anise
2 bay leaves
250g/9oz Greek yogurt
250g/9oz potatoes, diced
140g/5oz carrots, diced
140g/5oz frozen peas
small bunch coriander, finely chopped

1 Drain the rice and cook in boiling salted water for 8 minutes. Drain and set aside.

2 Heat the oil in a pan. Fry the onions until golden. Remove half the onions; set aside. Fry the rest until crisp. Drain; set aside.

3 Return the first batch of onions to the pan. Fry with the ginger and garlic for 1 minute, then stir in the tomatoes, spices, bay leaves, yogurt and some salt. Cook for a few minutes until the oil separates out. Add the potatoes, carrots and 400ml/14fl oz water. Gently cook for 20–30 minutes (splash in more water if it looks too thick). Turn off the heat and stir in the peas.

4 Spread half the cooked rice over the base of a large casserole with a lid. Spread the vegetables on top, sprinkle with coriander, then cover with the remaining rice. Dampen a thick tea towel, lay it over the casserole and put on the lid. Cook over a very low heat for 30 minutes. Spoon into a dish, mixing the vegetables and rice. Scatter over the crispy onions.

PER SERVING 562 kcals, protein 12g, carbs 79g, fat 24g, sat fat 5g, fibre 6g, sugar 12g, salt 0.14g

Fennel & roast-tomato lasagne

The fennel adds a fabulous flavour to this lasagne. Serve with some green salad leaves and crusty bread to complete this supper for friends.

TAKES 1 HOUR 5 MINUTES

● **SERVES 4**

3 fennel bulbs, sliced

3 tbsp extra virgin rapeseed oil

800g/1lb 12oz tomatoes on the vine

2 tbsp balsamic vinegar

150ml/¼ pint double cream, plus a dribble extra if needed

100g/4oz vegetarian Parmesan-style cheese

250g/9oz dried lasagne sheets

1 Heat the oven to 180C/160C fan/gas 4. Put the fennel in a large roasting tin, season and drizzle with 2 tablespoons of oil. Put the tomatoes on the vine in a separate roasting tin, season and drizzle with the remaining oil and the vinegar. Roast both tins of veg for 30 minutes.

2 Stir the cream into the fennel and return it to the oven for 10 minutes. Meanwhile, remove the vines from the roasted tomatoes, then lightly mash the flesh. After 10 minutes, remove the fennel from the oven, grate over most of cheese and stir to melt – it should make a little sauce that clings to the fennel a bit (add a dribble more cream, if you need to). Reduce the oven to 160C/140C fan/gas 3.

3 Spoon a thin layer of mashed tomatoes into a dish. Top with a layer of pasta, followed by a layer of fennel, then another layer of pasta. Repeat, finishing with a layer of fennel. Grate over the remaining cheese and bake for 45 minutes.

PER SERVING 626 kcals, protein 17g, carbs 57g, fat 39g, sat fat 17g, fibre 7g, sugar 12g, salt 0.54g

Thai red vegetable curry

Making your own Thai red curry paste tastes fabulous, but if time is short you can use readymade – just make sure it's suitable for vegetarians.

TAKES 50 MINUTES • SERVES 4

2 red chillies
4–5 tbsp soy sauce
juice 3 limes
200g/7oz firm tofu, cubed
2 tbsp vegetable oil
400ml can reduced-fat coconut milk
1 courgette, chopped into chunks
1 small aubergine, chopped into chunks
½ red pepper, roughly chopped
140g/5oz mushrooms, halved
140g/5oz sugar snap peas
20g pack basil, leaves picked
1 tsp brown sugar
jasmine rice, to serve

FOR THE PASTE

½ red pepper, roughly chopped
3 red chillies
1 lemongrass stalk, roughly chopped
3 shallots, roughly chopped
zest 1 lime
stalks from 20g pack coriander
thumb-size piece ginger, grated
2 garlic cloves
1 tsp each freshly ground pepper
    and coriander

1 Whizz the paste ingredients in a food processor.

2 Finely chop one chilli; slice the other into rounds. Mix together 2 tablespoons of the soy sauce, juice 1 lime and the chopped chilli. Add the tofu and leave to marinate.

3 Heat half the oil in a large pan. Add 3–4 tablespoons of the paste and fry for 2 minutes. Stir in the coconut milk with 100ml/3½fl oz water, the courgette, aubergine and red pepper, and cook for 10 minutes until almost tender.

4 Drain the tofu, pat dry, then fry in the remaining oil in a small pan until golden.

5 Add the mushrooms, sugar snaps and most of the basil to the curry, then season with the sugar, remaining lime juice and soy sauce. Cook for 4 minutes until the mushrooms are tender, then add the tofu and heat through. Scatter with the sliced chilli and remaining basil, and serve with jasmine rice.

PER SERVING 233 kcals, protein 8g, carbs 11g, fat 18g, sat fat 10g, fibre 3g, sugar 7g, salt 3.06g

Roasted-squash risotto with Wensleydale

The flavours really complement each other in this rich, creamy risotto, and the squash and cheese make a delicious combination. Any sort of squash or pumpkin works well.

TAKES 1¼ HOURS • SERVES 4

about 1kg/2lb 4oz peeled, deseeded
    squash, cubed
1 tbsp olive oil
handful pumpkin seeds
1 onion, chopped
1 garlic clove, crushed
25g/1oz butter
300g/10oz risotto rice
150ml/¼ pint white wine
1.2 litres/2 pints hot vegetable stock
100g/4oz Wensleydale cheese,
    crumbled
small bunch chives, snipped

1 Heat oven to 200C/180C fan/gas 6. Toss the squash in the oil in a roasting tin and roast for 15–20 minutes until tender and golden. With 4–5 minutes to go, toss the pumpkin seeds with a little salt, make a little space among the squash and spread out the seeds, then finish roasting. Remove half the squash and purée or mash it – keep the rest warm in a very low oven.

2 Meanwhile, soften the onion and garlic in the butter in a frying pan. Stir in the rice for 1–2 minutes. Add the wine and cook, stirring, until the alcohol has evaporated. Add the hot stock, a ladleful at a time, stirring until each addition is almost completely absorbed. Once all the stock has been added, the rice should be tender and creamy. Stir in the puréed or mashed squash until warm and season, if you like.

3 Serve in shallow bowls, scatter over the reserved roasted squash, the crumbled cheese, chives and pumpkin seeds.

PER SERVING 584 kcals, protein 17g, carbs 87g, fat 20g, sat fat 9g, fibre 8g, sugar 17g, salt 1.21g

Fennel & chestnut loaf with cranberry relish

A modern take on the traditional nut loaf. The cranberry-and-orange relish adds a tasty and colourful lift to the loaf.

TAKES 1¼ HOURS • SERVES 2

125g pack cooked chestnuts
6 juniper berries, squashed
1 tbsp sunflower oil, plus extra for greasing
1 onion, chopped
140g/5oz fennel, chopped
2 tsp thyme leaves
2 tsp orange zest
125ml/4fl oz orange juice
50g/2oz wholemeal breadcrumbs
25g/1oz ground almonds
50ml/2fl oz white wine
1 egg, beaten

FOR THE CRANBERRY RELISH

140g/5oz fresh or frozen cranberries
75g/2½oz granulated sugar
1 orange, segmented

1 Put the chestnuts and juniper berries in a small pan and just cover with water. Bring to the boil then remove from heat, cover and leave to infuse until cool. Once cool, drain the chestnuts and discard the berries. Meanwhile, heat the oil in a pan and fry the onion until soft. Add the fennel and cook for 3–4 minutes.

2 Heat oven to 180C/160C fan/gas 4. Grease a 1lb loaf tin with oil. Transfer the onion and fennel mixture to a mixing bowl and stir in the chestnuts and remaining ingredients with some seasoning. Spoon into the tin, smooth the top and cook for 35–40 minutes. Leave to cool for a few minutes in the tin before removing.

3 Put the cranberries in a pan and pour over 150ml/¼ pint water. Bring to the boil and cook until soft. Reduce the heat and add the sugar. Simmer until the mixture has thickened. Remove from the heat and allow to cool. Add the orange segments and serve the relish with the loaf.

PER SERVING 581 kcals, protein 13g, carbs 91g, fat 20g, sat fat 3g, fibre 11g, sugar 60g, salt 0.32g

Vegetable stew with herby dumplings

The pearl barley makes this stew really hearty. If you make it ahead, the barley will absorb all the sauce, so you'll need to splash in some more stock.

TAKES 2 HOURS 10 MINUTES

● **SERVES 6**

1 tbsp olive oil
350g/12oz shallots
2 leeks, thickly sliced
½ swede, peeled and chopped into chunks
2 parsnips, peeled and quartered
350g/12oz Chantenay carrots
175g/6oz pearl barley
225ml/8fl oz white wine
1 litre/1¾ pints vegetable stock
1 bay leaf
3 thyme sprigs
small bunch parsley, finely chopped

FOR THE DUMPLINGS

100g/4oz self-raising flour
50g/2oz unsalted butter
50g/2oz mature Cheddar, grated
2 tsp finely chopped rosemary
1 tsp thyme leaves

1 Heat the oil in a large casserole dish. Add the shallots and cook for 5–6 minutes until starting to soften and brown. Add the leeks for 2 minutes, then stir in the swede, parsnips and carrots.

2 Pour in the barley and wine, and cook until the liquid has reduced by half. Add the stock, bay leaf, thyme, parsley and some seasoning. Cover the pan, bring to the boil, then simmer for 45 minutes until the barley and veg are tender. Stir occasionally to stop it catching.

3 Meanwhile, make the dumplings. Heat oven to 200C/180C fan/gas 6. Rub the flour and butter together to form breadcrumbs. Add the remaining ingredients and mix well. Sprinkle over 2 tablespoons cold water and mix to form a soft dough. Divide into six and roll into balls. Dot on top of the stew and transfer to the oven. Cook, uncovered, for 20–25 minutes until the dumplings are golden.

PER SERVING 391 kcals, protein 10g, carbs 57g, fat 14g, sat fat 7g, fibre 8g, sugar 16g, salt 0.83g

Asparagus coconut crêpes with sweet chilli sauce

A truly fabulous flavour combination and the subtle coconut crêpes, spicy sweet chilli sauce and refreshing mint also make an eye-catching, elegant main course.

TAKES 50 MINUTES • SERVES 4

FOR THE CRÊPES

4 rounded tbsp plain flour

3 eggs, beaten

100ml/3½fl oz coconut milk

½ tsp ground turmeric

4 tsp sunflower oil

4 spring onions, finely sliced

2 bunches asparagus (about 20 spears), trimmed

2 eggs, hardboiled and chopped

FOR THE SAUCE

4 tbsp golden syrup or clear honey

4 tbsp light soy sauce

4 tbsp lime juice

2–4 red chillies, finely chopped

1 garlic clove, crushed

50g/2oz salted roasted peanuts, ground with a mortar and pestle

TO SERVE

1 cucumber, thinly sliced

small bunch mint sprigs

1 To make the sauce, mix together the syrup or honey, soy sauce and lime juice until smooth. Stir in the chillies and garlic. Transfer to a serving bowl and sprinkle in the peanuts. Set aside.

2 Make the crêpes: stir the flour, eggs, coconut milk, turmeric and some seasoning together until smooth. Heat a non-stick frying pan over a medium heat and add 1 teaspoon of the oil. Pour in a quarter of the batter in a thin layer and swirl the pan so it coats the base. Sprinkle with a quarter of the spring onions before it sets. When golden underneath, flip over and cook the other side. Remove to a plate and keep warm. Make three more crêpes.

3 Steam the asparagus for 3–5 minutes. Divide the asparagus and eggs into four portions. Put a bundle of asparagus on a crêpe, sprinkle with egg, then roll up and cut in half on the diagonal. Serve with a garnish of cucumber and a mint sprig, with the sauce spooned over or on the side.

PER SERVING 383 kcals, protein 17g, carbs 30g, fat 22g, sat fat 7g, fibre 4g, sugar 17g, salt 3.23g

Spinach & ricotta cannelloni

This is a great dish to serve for supper with friends, or you can it eat now and freeze half uncooked for another day. If freezing, thaw overnight and cook as below.

TAKES 1½ HOURS • SERVES 10

FOR THE TOMATO SAUCE
3 tbsp olive oil
8 garlic cloves, crushed
3 tbsp caster sugar
2 tbsp red wine vinegar
4 × 400g cans chopped tomatoes
small bunch basil leaves

FOR THE TOPPING
2 × 250g tubs mascarpone
3 tbsp milk
85g/3oz vegetarian Parmesan-style cheese, grated
2 × 125g balls mozzarella, sliced

FOR THE FILLING
1kg/2lb 4oz spinach leaves
100g/4oz vegetarian Parmesan-style cheese, grated
3 × 250g tubs ricotta
large pinch grated nutmeg
400g/14oz dried cannelloni

1 Heat the oil in a pan and fry the garlic for 1 minute. Add the sugar, vinegar, tomatoes and some seasoning. Simmer for 20 minutes, stirring occasionally, until thick. Add the basil and put the sauce into one or two shallow dishes. Set aside.

2 Make a sauce for the topping by beating the mascarpone with the milk until smooth, season, then set aside.

3 For the filling, put the spinach in a colander and pour over boiling water to wilt it. When cool enough, squeeze out the excess water. Chop the spinach; mix it with the grated cheese and ricotta. Season with salt, pepper and nutmeg.

4 Heat oven to 200C/180C fan/gas 6. Using a piping bag, squeeze the filling into cannelloni tubes. Lay the tubes, side by side, on top of the tomato sauce and spoon over the mascarpone sauce. Top with grated cheese and mozzarella. Bake for 30–35 minutes. Remove from the oven and let stand for 5 minutes before serving.

PER SERVING 711 kcals, protein 30g, carbs 44g, fat 47g, sat fat 27g, fibre 5g, sugar 15g, salt 1.59g

Chickpea & roasted-veg tagine

This Moroccan-style stew tastes even better if made a few hours or even a day in advance. Any leftovers can be reheated or frozen.

TAKES 1 HOUR 10 MINUTES

● **SERVES 6**

350g/12oz new potatoes, halved

1 fennel bulb, trimmed and cut into chunks

1 medium carrot, cut into chunks

1 red or yellow pepper, deseeded and cut into chunks

1 large red onion, cut into chunks

4 tbsp rapeseed or extra virgin olive oil

1 tsp cumin seeds

1 tsp fennel seeds

1 tsp coriander seeds, crushed

3 garlic cloves, chopped

400g can chopped tomatoes

400g can chickpeas, rinsed and drained

250ml/9fl oz red wine

zest and juice 1 orange

1 cinnamon stick

8 prunes, halved

couscous and a scattering of toasted flaked almonds, to serve (optional)

1 Heat oven to 220C/200C fan/gas 7. Put the potatoes, fennel, carrot, pepper and onion in a roasting tin with 3 tablespoons of the oil, the cumin, fennel and coriander seeds, and some salt and pepper. Use your hands to coat everything, then roast for 30 minutes, stirring once, until tinged golden brown and the potatoes are cooked through.

2 Meanwhile, heat a large pan over a medium heat and add the remaining 1 tablespoon of the oil. Fry the garlic until fragrant, then add the tomatoes, chickpeas, wine, orange zest and juice, cinnamon and prunes. Bring to the boil and simmer while the vegetables roast.

3 Add the roasted vegetables to the pan and stir. Return to a simmer and cook for 15–20 minutes. Serve over warm couscous scattered with toasted flaked almonds, if using.

PER SERVING 241 kcals, protein 7g, carbs 32g, fat 9g, sat fat 1g, fibre 5g, sugar 15g, salt 0.36g

Melanzane lasagne

The aubergines add a lovely texture to this lasagne. It can be frozen uncooked and then thawed overnight. Serve with crisp salad leaves and crusty bread.

TAKES 1 HOUR 10 MINUTES
● **SERVES 4**

3 aubergines, sliced lengthways
2 tbsp olive oil
3 large garlic cloves, crushed
680ml jar passata
½ tbsp dried oregano
1 tsp sugar
1 tbsp red wine vinegar
small bunch basil leaves, torn
100g/4oz vegetarian Parmesan-style
   cheese, grated
125g ball mozzarella, torn
200g/7oz fresh lasagne sheets
5 tbsp breadcrumbs
salad leaves and crusty bread, to serve

1 Heat grill to high. Arrange the aubergine slices on a baking sheet, brush with some of the oil and season well. Grill for 2–3 minutes each side until golden brown and set aside.

2 Heat the remaining oil in a pan. Fry the garlic for 1 minute then pour in the passata. Simmer for 10 minutes with the oregano, sugar and vinegar, then season and stir in the basil.

3 Heat oven to 200C/180C fan/gas 6. Assemble the lasagne in a roughly A4-sized baking dish. Spread a few tablespoons of the tomato sauce over the base of the dish, followed by a layer of aubergine. Scatter over some Parmesan and mozzarella, then cover with a layer of lasagne. Repeat, finishing with a topping of cheese, and sprinkle on the breadcrumbs. Cook the lasagne for 25–30 minutes until golden brown and bubbling.

PER SERVING 460 kcals, protein 24g, carbs 44g, fat 22g, sat fat 10g, fibre 6g, sugar 11g, salt 1.99g

Fried coconut bananas

Palm sugar has a rich flavour and is often used in Thai cooking. It is available from the special ingredients sections in stores. Soft light brown sugar can be used instead.

TAKES 20 MINUTES ● SERVES 2

2 tbsp palm sugar or soft light brown
   sugar
2 bananas, peeled, halved lengthways,
   then each chunk halved again
150ml/¼ pint coconut milk
coconut ice cream, to serve
toasted shredded coconut, to scatter

1 Heat the sugar in a small frying pan. When melted, add the bananas and caramelise on each side for 3–4 minutes. Lift out and set aside.

2 Tip the coconut milk into the pan with a pinch of salt, stir into the sugar and bubble until syrupy. Divide between two bowls, top with the caramelised bananas, then add a scoop of ice cream and scatter with toasted coconut.

PER SERVING 272 kcals, protein 2g, carbs 40g, fat 13g, sat fat 11g, fibre 1g, sugar 38g, salt 0.22g

Easy gooseberry cobbler

Gooseberries are one of the few fruits that retain much of their vitamin C levels when cooked. Plums or damsons can also be used in this low-fat recipe.

TAKES 40 MINUTES • SERVES 6

750g/1lb 10oz gooseberries, topped, tailed and washed

100g/4oz caster sugar

1 tsp grated root ginger

3 tbsp elderflower cordial

low-fat ice cream, fromage frais or custard, to serve

FOR THE TOPPING

140g/5oz plain flour

2 tsp baking powder

25g/1oz butter

25g/1oz caster sugar

150ml/¼ pint buttermilk

1 tbsp demerara sugar

1 Heat oven to 190C/170C fan/gas 5. Put the gooseberries, caster sugar, ginger and elderflower cordial in a pan with 4 tablespoons water and cook, covered, for 5 minutes until the gooseberries begin to pop. Tip into a baking dish.

2 Make the topping. Sift the flour, baking powder and a pinch of salt into a mixing bowl. Rub in the butter until the mixture looks like breadcrumbs, then stir in the caster sugar. Mix in the buttermilk to give a soft, sticky dough. Dollop spoonfuls on top of the gooseberries, then sprinkle with the demerara. Bake for 25 minutes or until golden brown and crusty. Stand for 5 minutes, then serve with some low-fat ice cream, fromage frais or custard.

PER SERVING 255 kcals, protein 5g, carbs 53g, fat 4g, sat fat 2g, fibre 4g, sugar 34g, salt 0.52g

Peach Melba knickerbocker glory

Kids will love this retro pud. Look out for white-fleshed peaches – they're sweeter than their yellow-fleshed cousins.

TAKES 30 MINUTES ● **MAKES 4**

300g/10oz raspberries
50g/2oz caster sugar
200ml/7fl oz double cream
4 ripe peaches, halved, stones
  removed
8 scoops good-quality vanilla ice cream
handful flaked almonds

1 Blitz half the raspberries with half the sugar and a splash of water to make a raspberry sauce, then tip into a small bowl and set aside.

2 In a separate bowl, whisk the cream with the remaining sugar until stiff and spoonable, then set aside. Thinly slice the peaches.

3 In four tall sundae glasses, layer the peach slices, remaining raspberries and the raspberry sauce, finishing with scoops of ice cream, a generous spoonful of whipped cream and a scattering of flaked almonds. Serve straight away with long spoons.

PER SUNDAE 498 kcals, protein 6g, carbs 38g, fat 37g, sat fat 19g, fibre 4g, sugar 37g, salt 0.13g

Roast apples with cinnamon sugar

Fabulous flavours drift from the oven with this leave-to-cook pud. Fluffy apples and a gorgeous sticky sauce just need a dollop of custard or a scoop of ice cream.

TAKES 1 HOUR • MAKES 6

75g/2½oz golden granulated sugar
¾ tsp ground cinnamon
50g/2oz natural dried breadcrumbs
8 dried apricots, roughly chopped
75g/2½oz butter, chopped
zest and juice 1 orange
6 large Bramley apples
custard or vanilla ice cream, to serve

1 Mix together the sugar and cinnamon, and set aside. Heat oven to 180C/160C fan/gas 4.

2 Mix together the breadcrumbs, apricots, cinnamon sugar, butter and orange zest.

3 Using an apple corer, remove the centre of each apple, then score the skin around the apples so they don't collapse during roasting.

4 Pack the filling into the apples, then sit them snugly in an ovenproof dish. Mix together the orange juice and 150ml/¼ pint water, and pour round the apples. Roast for 40–50 minutes until nicely browned and very soft, but still just holding their shape. Serve with the sticky pan juices and custard or ice cream.

PER APPLE 246 kcals, protein 2g, carbs 38g, fat 11g, sat fat 7g, fibre 3g, sugar 32g, salt 0.26g

Oaty apple crumble

This recipe makes two crumbles – one to eat now and one to freeze for another day.
The combination of cooking and eating apples gives a good sweet – tart balance.

TAKES 1 HOUR 40 MINUTES
- **SERVES 10**

6 Bramley apples, peeled, cored and
   cut into chunks
6 eating apples, peeled, cored and
   cut into chunks
85g/3oz caster sugar
100g/4oz sultanas or raisins
100g/4oz soft light brown sugar
50g/2oz honey
250g pack butter
300g/10oz oats
300g/10oz plain flour
100g/4oz flaked almonds
1 tsp ground cinnamon

1 Cook the apples with the caster sugar in a large pan, stirring occasionally – add a splash of water if they start to stick on the bottom. When just about tender and a bit saucy, stir in the sultanas or raisins and tip into two large ovenproof dishes.

2 Melt the brown sugar, honey and butter together in a large pan. Off the heat, stir in the oats, flour, almonds and cinnamon until sticky and crumbly. Divide the mixture over the apples. To bake straight away, heat oven to 180C/160C fan/gas 4 and cook for 40–50 minutes until the topping is golden and crisp.

3 Freeze the other dish, well wrapped, and cook from frozen, covered with foil, at 180C/160C fan/gas 4 for 1½ hours, then turn the oven up to 220C/200C fan/gas 7 and bake for a further 45 minutes, removing the foil for the last 15 minutes.

PER SERVING 646 kcals, protein 11g, carbs 91g,
fat 29g, sat fat 14g, fibre 8g, sugar 48g,
salt 0.48g

Almond & apricot trifles

If you don't want to use alcohol in this simple pud, replace the Disaronno with 8 tablespoons more of the apricot juice mixed with 1 teaspoon almond extract.

TAKES 10 MINUTES • MAKES 4

1 shop-bought Madeira loaf cake, cut into cubes
8 tbsp Disaronno liqueur
2 × 410g cans apricots, chopped and juice reserved
500g pot fresh custard
300ml/½ pint double cream
2 tbsp toasted flaked almonds

1 Line the bottom of four small glass serving dishes with the cake. Mix half the Disaronno with 6 tablespoons of reserved apricot juice, then divide this among the bowls. Arrange the apricots on top of the sponge, then pour on the custard. Cover and chill for at least 10 minutes, or up to a day.

2 Just before serving, add the remaining Disaronno to the cream and whip until it just holds its shape. Spoon the cream over the custard and sprinkle with toasted flaked almonds.

PER TRIFLE 1,017 kcals, protein 10g, carbs 99g, fat 62g, sat fat 34g, fibre 3g, sugar 77g, salt 0.97g

Baked lemon & vanilla rice pudding

Always a favourite with the family, the uplifting zing of lemon zest cuts through the richness of this comforting classic. Perfect for a Sunday lunch pud.

TAKES 1 HOUR 40 MINUTES
- **SERVES 4–6**

600ml/1 pint milk
450ml/16fl oz single cream
zest 1 lemon
1 vanilla pod, split
25g/1oz caster sugar
100g/4oz pudding rice
25g/1oz butter, diced

1 Heat oven to 140C/120C fan/gas 1. Put the milk, cream, lemon zest and vanilla pod in a pan. Gently bring to a simmer, then stir in the caster sugar and rice.

2 Pour the mixture into a shallow ovenproof dish and dot the butter on top. Bake for 30 minutes, then stir well and cook for 1 hour more until the pudding is soft and creamy and a golden skin has formed on top. The depth and type of dish you use will affect the cooking time, so if the pudding seems too loose, return it to the oven and check every 10 minutes or so. Once cooked, leave the pudding to rest for 10 minutes before serving.

PER SERVING (6) 309 kcals, protein 6g, carbs 27g, fat 20g, sat fat 12g, fibre none, sugar 10g, salt none

Blueberry & coconut pudding

This coconut-and lemon-flavoured sponge pudding is quick to make, and the ingredients can be easily doubled so it serves all the family.

TAKES 1 HOUR ● SERVES 2

50g/2oz caster sugar
50g/2oz soft butter
1 large egg
50g/2oz self-raising flour
50g/2oz desiccated coconut, plus 2 tsp
   to scatter
50g/2oz crème fraîche, plus extra
   to serve
zest and juice 1 lemon
180g punnet blueberries

1 Heat oven to 180C/160C fan/gas 4. Beat the sugar and butter until pale and creamy, then beat in the egg. Stir in the flour, coconut, crème fraîche and lemon zest.

2 Put most of the blueberries in a baking dish (about 18cm square-ish) and squeeze over the juice from half the lemon. Dollop on the cake mixture and scatter over the remaining blueberries and the extra 2 teaspoons coconut. Bake for 35–40 minutes until golden, risen and the sponge is cooked. Serve with a dollop more crème fraîche.

PER SERVING 708 kcals, protein 9g, carbs 54g, fat 52g, sat fat 36g, fibre 6g, sugar 36g, salt 0.68g

Lemon curd & raspberry pots

A superfast lemony version of the traditional Eton Mess pud. Strawberries or blueberries would also be good, or use a mixture of fruit.

TAKES 10 MINUTES • MAKES 4
300ml pot double cream
140g punnet raspberries
4 tbsp lemon curd
4 large meringue nests, roughly
  crushed

1 Whip the cream until stiff. Gently fold in about three-quarters of the raspberries, plus the lemon curd and meringue so that some of the berries break up and some remain whole, and there is a ripple effect.

2 Divide the mixture among four bowls and dot over the remaining raspberries.

PER POT 478 kcals, protein 2g, carbs 26g, fat 41g, sat fat 23g, fibre 1g, sugar 23g, salt 0.11g

Peach & almond slices

The chopped marzipan adds an unexpected dimension to the flavour of this pud. Nectarines, plums or greengages can also be used.

TAKES 30 MINUTES • MAKES 6

375g pack ready-rolled puff pastry
flour, for dusting
1 egg, beaten
175g/6oz marzipan, chopped
3 peaches, halved, stoned and thinly
   sliced
1 tbsp flaked almonds
crème fraîche, to serve

1 Heat oven to 220C/200C fan/gas 7. Unroll the pastry on a lightly floured surface and cut in half horizontally. Slice each half into three squares.

2 Lay the pastry sheets on a baking sheet. Use a knife to mark a 1cm/½in border on each – be careful not to go all the way through the pastry. Prick inside the border with a fork, then brush all over with beaten egg.

3 Bake for 10 minutes until golden and slightly risen. Divide the marzipan equally among the pastry squares and fan out the peach slices on top, followed by a sprinkling of almonds.

4 Put the slices back into the oven for 10 minutes until they have puffed up and are golden. Serve with a dollop of crème fraîche.

PER SLICE 408 kcals, protein 7g, carbs 42g, fat 25g, sat fat 8g, fibre 2g, sugar 25g, salt 0.69g

Index